'A rich, thoughtful book that will be of great help to incumbents, missioners, planters, pioneers, innovators and senior leaders. Ed's heart for the church and its mission – along with a generosity that enables the whole body to be joined together and mutually supportive in its ecosystem – shines through.'
Jonny Baker, CMS Britain Hub mission director

'Ed is a master of the metaphor. Here he adds depth and complexity to what has proved to be the incredibly generative image of the mixed ecology in churches. Ed recognises the inherent problems with the image as well as what it promises. As such, this is a valuable contribution to the conversations about what we think the church might look like in the coming decades.'
The Revd Dr Will Foulger, Vicar of St Nics, Durham

'In a society where culture is anything but homogenous, we need multiple methods of engaging with those who, when it comes to Christian faith, are 'not sure', 'doubtful', 'maybes' and 'sort ofs' . . . Ed explores, in creative, visual and attractive ways, a mixed ecology approach which is coherent, culturally savvy and adaptable to a wide variety of contexts in worship and witness. This is a rich and helpful resource.'
The Rt Revd Dr Mike Harrison, Bishop of Dunwich

'Wise, generous and invigorating, Ed Olsworth-Peter's exceptional volume is a gift to the church.'
The Rt Revd Dr Emma Ineson, Bishop of Kensington

'This is a beautiful book about connectivity, conversations and collaborations. It helps us see the church as a living ecosystem and encourages us to let it grow. Images and ideas abound for practitioners to imagine and then create a church of diverse praise.'
The Revd Dr Victoria Johnson, Dean of Chapel, St John's College, Cambridge and member of The College of Archbishops' Evangelists

'What a treat of a read, full of vivid and varied illustrations to bring the points home and studded with fascinating insights from contemporary thinkers an~~d~~ warm enthusiasm and gentle

generosity to this timely exploration of what mixed ecology can be at its best.'
Lucy Moore, Head of the Growing Faith Foundation and founder of Messy Church

'Too often, being a broad church means keeping our distance from the Christian communities which are different from ours. *Mixed Ecology* by Ed Olsworth-Peter is a powerful and timely reminder that every expression of church – every variety of time-honoured and new worshipping communities – not only has a place in the Church of England, but will better serve the mission of God by embracing their interconnectedness and interdependence with one another. This book, itself a product of diverse voices, has valuable and practical wisdom for church leaders of any tradition or ministry.'
The Rt Revd Saju Muthalaly, Bishop of Loughborough

'Ed Olsworth-Peter is the sympathetic ecologist we need to imagine a healthy and diverse future for the church. In this creative contribution, he offers valuable models and methods practitioners will need to get there. I love the way Ed is such a generous host, giving voice to a fascinating range of conversation partners along the way. Read this accessible book to explore the why and how of mixed ecology – its value and the virtues that make it flourish – and to find yourself on the map unfolding before us.'
The Revd Canon Dr Mark Powley, Archbishop's Mission Enabler for the North

'We live in a season when the Holy Spirit is inspiring a range of forms of Christian community to connect with neighbours where they are. One size, shape, or model of church isn't sufficient; we need many, working together. Ed Olsworth-Peter's *Mixed Ecology* explores this terrain with wisdom, insight, and practical advice for leaders at all levels of the church. This is a very hopeful book.'
Dwight Zscheile, Vice President of Innovation and Professor of Congregational Mission and Leadership, Luther Seminary, St Paul, Minnesota

MIXED ECOLOGY

Ed Olsworth-Peter is Director of Innovation and Development at St Mellitus Theological College where he teaches on missional ecclesiology, mixed ecology, Pioneer ministry and ministry discernment. He is an experienced conference speaker and has delivered talks nationally and internationally. He was previously the National Adviser for Pioneer Development for the Church of England, responsible for implementing and overseeing a strategy for the vocation, training and deployment of lay and ordained pioneers. Ed has been ordained since 2004 and has been a parish priest, a pioneer minister, a diocesan adviser and a theatre chaplain in London's West End.

MIXED ECOLOGY

Inhabiting an integrated church

Ed Olsworth-Peter

First published in Great Britain in 2024

SPCK
SPCK Group
Studio 101 The Record Hall
16–16A Baldwin's Gardens
London EC1N 7RJ
www.spckpublishing.co.uk

British Library Cataloguing-in-Publication Data
A catalogue record for this book is available from the British Library

ISBN 978-0-2810-8937-6
eBook ISBN 978-0-2810-8938-3

Typeset by Fakenham Prepress Solutions, Fakenham, Norfolk NR21 8NL
Printed in Great Britain by Clays Ltd, Bungay, Suffolk

eBook by Fakenham Prepress Solutions, Fakenham, Norfolk NR21 8NL

Produced on paper from sustainable forests

Contents

Introduction

For the Church to grow it needs to embrace the value of co-growing different expressions of Church and missional activity alongside one another. By maintaining their distinctness and living in active relationship they can benefit the mutual growth of the missional and ecclesial kingdom of God.[1]

This statement sums up the focus of this book and the research I have been doing on the mixed ecology of church for nearly ten years. A key theme within this is 'connectivity': connectivity in the life of the church, in the discipleship of its people and in the communities it seeks to reach; connectivity that breaks down unhealthy competition, that allows for a richer flow of information and ideas, and which gives increased confidence to share who Jesus is. Within my own denomination of the Church of England, a new strategy has been launched calling for the 'mixed ecology of church to be the norm' and for the church to be humbler, simpler and bolder.[2] Judging from my experience, I think this echoes the desire and lived experience of many local churches, but if it is to become more of a reality, the church will need to go on a journey of discovery as it responds to what this truly means.

In 2023, I had the privilege of leading the ordination retreat for the Diocese of Lichfield. Tradition dictates that the Retreat Conductor preaches at the ordination services. I'm ordained and a pioneer often advocating for innovation, and so as I climbed the many steps up to the pulpit in the cathedral – wearing a very ornate red and gold cope and stole – there was a whiff of the mixed ecology in the air! The New Testament reading set for the service was Matthew chapter 16, where Jesus, in response to Peter's realisation that he is the Messiah, declares, 'And I tell you that you are Peter, and on this rock I will build my church' (Matthew 16:18, NIV). The Greek version of Peter is 'Petros', which can

1

also be translated as 'little stone', and the Greek word for rock is 'petra', which can also be translated as boulder,[3] so there is an amusing play on words here. My main point was that in some ways Jesus is saying, 'You are a little stone but on this boulder I will build my church.' My own view is that the boulder Jesus is referring to is what Peter will become, a person of great sacrificial faith, but that the faith Peter demonstrates here as he declares Jesus' identity is something that all followers should aspire to in order for the church to be built. I went on to explain that, even in our smallness, we can do amazing and challenging things through our God-given, boulder-like faith. There are some resonances here with the book of 1 Peter, where the writer refers to those of faith being living stones and building the church, together with Christ, the cornerstone (1 Peter 2:4–6). So, if the church is made up of a multitude of little stones, I don't think its growth will come about through a few big boulder-like initiatives. It will be through lots of smaller church and missional activity, scattered everywhere, performed in a simpler and humbler way, connected and integrated in a community or ecosystem, and achieved by the boulder-like faith of everyone. This is the mixed ecology.

As a society, we have a curious relationship with connectivity. Digital media means we have never been more connected. I think most of my immediate family would scarcely hear from me if it weren't for the helpful prompt messages on our various family WhatsApp groups. And yet we still find it hard to start up a conversation on the daily commute or when queuing at the post office, and isolation and loneliness remain huge problems in our society. I don't think the church has really got the importance of connectivity either. The Churches Together and ecumenical movements have done much to form relationships across denominations, and yet I remember being in a meeting of pioneers in East Anglia a few years back and introducing to each other two pioneers who lived a mile apart: they had never met, as they were part of different church communities.

Our missiological and ecclesiological landscape is becoming increasingly diverse, and as we respond to the call of God and the needs of the world, we will require a variety of approaches. There are time-honoured (also referred to as 'inherited') churches that have been present for many generations; there are established planting and pioneering networks; there are secular and institutional chaplaincies; there are new expressions of church that seek to draw people to them or dwell incarnationally within the missional landscape; there are missional entrepreneurs (sometimes referred to as community activists[4]) who are engaged in income-generating, self-supporting mission projects; there are evangelists ... I could go on. The church has always been diverse as it has evolved and changed over time, but now it needs to celebrate and cultivate diversity in a greater way and as one body.

Brighton on the south coast of England is famous for having two piers: the West Pier, built in 1866, and the Brighton, or Palace, Pier, built in 1899.[5] The Palace Pier is still in good condition. It attracts many locals and tourists to enjoy food, views and the thrills and spills of the funfair at its far end. In contrast, just down the beach, the West Pier is considered to be beyond repair after numerous fires. As a listed building, however, it cannot be demolished, and so is slowly rusting and disintegrating into the sea. Piers were traditionally built for a number of purposes, initially for fishing, but as time went on they provided an access point from the sea to the land in places where boats couldn't land on the shore owing to shallow water. When boats and steamships, often carrying goods and tourists, were the fastest way to navigate round the British Isles, any seaside town that didn't have a pier was at a disadvantage. With the introduction of the railways, this became less important. Another purpose of a pier was to provide entertainment: they offered hospitality, music and theatre and were a place for the aspiring classes to socialise, to be 'seen'. Piers also offered escapism, inviting people on a journey out over the water towards the horizon, the 'other', while providing an opportunity to observe the land behind from a different perspective.[6]

Today, the West Pier is no more than a rusting iron structure, but there are a few interesting things to notice. First, although the wooden platform between land and sea has gone, the cathedral-like columns that held up the pier remain. On the seafront, a piece of art has been created by repurposing some of these columns to create a walkway and a point for meeting and socialising. The columns are arranged in a spiral, almost like a nautical labyrinth. A new column has been constructed, however, a 160-metre-high steel structure on which a viewing platform ascends and descends.[7] The British Airways i360 – known locally as 'the doughnut' – provides a new way of exploring 'the other' beyond the land, by means of a vertical rather than a horizontal journey. It stands in the centre of the original gateway to the West Pier, almost as a new incarnation of what has gone before.

You could regard Brighton seafront as an ecosystem of different attractions, and it provides a useful metaphor for the mixed ecology. The Palace Pier is an example of something time-honoured that still has value and purpose. The West Pier could be likened to a past expression of church: one in decline, lacking its former impact and role. It is an uncomfortable truth that inherited and legal structures – or simply a desire to preserve what once was in the hope that it can be restored – at times prevent the acceptance of inevitable closure. This may be owing to external influences, such as changing social patterns or something like the Covid-19 pandemic causing a damaging 'fire to burn through the building'. And yet 'columns' – whether founding values, or the historic story of a community, or a spiritual and theological legacy – may be drawn on to create something new: perhaps a new monastic expression of church, or one of the many fresh expressions that have sprung from the time-honoured church.

The fact that the i360 is built at the entrance to the old West Pier acknowledges the importance of traditional entry points into new things. In the church, life events (weddings, baptisms and funerals) and festivals such as Christmas still bring people over the threshold and can be a pathway into new expressions of church within a mixed ecology. The old and the new can work together. The ticket booths of the original pier are now a café, drawing on Brighton's fashionable vintage culture. Though some locals think the pier should be allowed to be put out of its misery, you might say it has become an important reminder of what was, now reimagined with a new hope.

Ecosystems

Ecosystems are everywhere. We might instinctively look to the natural world to see different organisms living alongside and relying on one another, but ecosystems are evident in other aspects of life too. Road traffic systems comprise a series of various static and moving parts that all depend on one another for roads to flow well. I sometimes delight in the dance of a well-ordered roundabout with vehicles moving on and off the roads, each giving way (I'm a geographer; don't judge me!). We also see ecosystems in the social dynamics of a family or group of friends operating and interacting, in business networks and throughout social media. All such ecosystems have connectivity at their heart: it's the glue or essential substance that holds them together. Where connectivity isn't present, these ecosystems will cease to function well and simply become an amalgamation of separate entities.

This book explores what an integrated mixed ecology of church looks like in a post-pandemic world. As society moves beyond the cultural and financial impact of the pandemic, the way we meet as churches and how we reach out to those within our communities need to be reconsidered. Much has been written about the mixed economy/ecology of church over the last fifteen years, across a range of traditions and denominations: what haven't been explored as much are the importance of connectivity and interdependence between different expressions of church and mission initiatives, and the value of 'co-growing' alongside one another for mutual health and development. More than ever, there is a need for the church to be 'one body', unified yet distinctive, aware of the gift of its breadth in a 'global' ecosystem that together recognises and resources different expressions of church.

Each chapter of this book explores a different aspect of the mixed ecology and ends with some questions for consideration. It aims to help church leaders and worshipping communities to understand their place within the mixed ecology, the value of growing their own local ecosystem, and how to develop a physically gathered, digital and hybrid ecology of church. Offering cultural, ecclesiological and missional insights, coupled with practical application, it draws on the voices of respected theologians, authors and church leaders in the UK and the US, with a small group of conversation partners sharing their thoughts at key 'talking-point' moments.

1

Why a mixed ecology?

So, what is the mixed ecology and why should it become the norm? To answer this, we need to go back to the early 2000s, when the then Archbishop of Canterbury, Rowan Williams, called for fresh expressions of church to be developed to serve the missional landscape of England. We are very privileged to have Bishop Rowan on staff at St Mellitus as McDonald Distinguished Emeritus Professor of Theology. I sat down with him to ask him more about the thinking behind this mandate. He recalls:

> It came from the foreword to the Church in Wales report *Good News in Wales*, written while I was Archbishop of Wales. It was picked up again a year or so later by Graham Cray in his introduction to *Mission-Shaped Church* in 2004. The idea was that although there was a place for the traditional church, there was also a call for a whole host of fresh expressions of church to respond to the missio Dei.[1]

The *Mission-Shaped Church* report was published in 2004[2] and challenged the church to become more mission-focused in its form, calling it to develop new 'fresh' expressions of church that would assist with this mandate. In truth, these existed before 2004, but the report set out a more focused intention. The twenty years that followed have seen the growth of an international fresh expressions and planting movement, licensed and trained lay and ordained pioneer ministers, lay and ordained church planters, and many conferences, webinars and books – all seeking to foster the development of different types of new Christian community.

Talking point

I was interested in learning what my conversation partners thought about the evolving language that has been part of this process, so I asked Beth Keith, Andrew Dunlop and Tim Yau, 'People talk about mixed economy, blended church, mixed ecology – are they just different ways of talking about the same thing?'

Beth: The term 'ecology' or 'ecosystem' gives much more as it uses imagery that is readily available and much more imaginable. I think 'ecosystem' is useful because it gives a picture of a more open or organic space in which different species grow and interact. Within that imagery, it's easy to see how different species might need different growing conditions, that some thrive together, and that some will compete and affect those nearby. It's an image that assumes diversity is beneficial and necessary, rather than a threat to the old order. It also emphasises the importance of relationship and interaction between differing species, and that they are ever-changing and evolving.

Andrew: I try to use the word that the people I'm speaking to will understand, which varies according to context. Since 2021, 'mixed ecology' has been the term in common use. This gives the idea of biodiversity – different elements all contributing something different towards one ecosystem. Jesus often used ecological metaphors to describe the kingdom. Previously, I would have used the term 'mixed economy', as that was the most understood. But because it uses the language of economics, the relational aspect of the new and traditional churches working together can be missed. 'Blended' was used in a couple of dioceses. In my mind, this gives the impression of everything being mushed up together into one new entity (like a smoothie), losing the distinctness of constituent ingredients and thus the individuality of the constituent churches or missional communities. Ecology or biodiversity is much better, as it preserves the identity of individual groups and the overall purpose of the whole church.[3]

Tim: The phrase 'mixed economy' made practitioners think of budgets, business and commerce, whereas we were trying to bring the church back to something more simple and organic. Therefore, it was no surprise when 'mixed ecology' was used instead. Imaginatively, ecology leaves more room for creative thinking than economy. Nothing is wasted in ecology; even dead things become a source of life for what comes next. Christian communities don't always go on for ever, and as a result they can become a seedbed for something new and equally beautiful. Mixed ecology is about diversity and mutual flourishing: one cannot live without the other; churches and missional communities need each other, the time-honoured *and* the emerging. So there's something there about the need for biodiversity to increase resilience that I think resonates well with the need for a mixed economy/ecology in the church.

My own journey within the mixed ecology

I was ordained in 2004, the same year that the *Mission-Shaped Church* report was published. In my last few months of training, I felt increasingly uncomfortable about this impending life change. I liked learning about ordination but wasn't as convinced that I actually wanted to do it! I remember clearly the experience of coming down to the chapel of the retreat centre before my ordination in my black clerical shirt, being greeted by fifteen other people also in black clerical shirts, and the reality hitting home. I was accompanied through the ordination service by my new training incumbent and members of my curacy parishes, my family, godparents, friends and people from other churches I'd been part of. Still uneasy, I got to the back of the cathedral and, after the final blessing from the bishop who had ordained me, had the overwhelming feeling I'd made a really big mistake. Not the best frame of mind in which to greet my many waiting supporters!

The next couple of years of soul searching were tricky, but eventually I realised that ordination hadn't been a mistake. It was just that the way I was to live out my calling within the church looked different from the traditional parish model. This isn't to say there is anything wrong with that model and, in fact, I went on to lead a number of parish churches. However, fundamentally, it isn't my shape.

In the years that followed, I went on to be a pioneer minister and a West End theatre chaplain working within the arts; more recently, I have taken on advisory or teaching roles in the area of pioneer ministry and innovation. As I've reflected on two decades of ministry, however, it's become clear that as well as having a love of starting new things and 'thinking outside the box', I also have a heart for the local, time-honoured church. As a child I was a server and a bell ringer (actually more fun and more complicated than the stereotypes would suggest!), growing up with Holy Communion from the Book of Common Prayer in a small Sussex village church. Part of my ordination calling was to support the growth and development of local churches such as this. So I am a bit of a hybrid in that I love the new and want to develop the old. And I'm not the only one. There are an increasing number of people who feel called to lead different expressions of church at the same time, in response to various needs in the missional context around them. Such people are becoming known as 'mixed ecology ministers', which is a phrase I have been using for a while. I think it came into public use through a Dave Walker cartoon published in the *Church Times* in 2021[4] in response to a piece of research I co-wrote called 'The Mixed Ecologists' (discussed later in this book).

There is something very important, then, about the relationship between the ancient and the future, the supposedly 'old' and the new. The more I have thought about this, the clearer it has become that both have value for the people of God. Each can inform the other. As an example, when I was working for the Diocese of Ely, a team of us were commissioned to start a new missional monastic community. The Community of St Etheldreda had existed for many years, formed out of the Benedictine foundation of Ely Cathedral, but we felt a call to draw on this ancient tradition for our contemporary age. We were given a beautiful chapel space in the Cathedral Close and prayed about what we could use it for. What emerged was really fascinating. After some experimentation, we realised that you could map the four vows of the St Etheldreda

Benedictine tradition (obedience, work, stability and transformation) onto the Fresh Expressions journey – a six-stage process for starting pioneering forms of church. These stages are: listening to God and the missional context; loving and serving the world around you; building community from this social action work; exploring faith over time as a community forms and ask questions; church taking shape in response to this, and reviewing what has formed or doing it again.[5] Here is what we discovered:

'Listening' is enhanced by the posture of 'obedience'. The Latin root of the word 'obedience' means *to listen intently to God.* This aids us in being responsive and faithful to what we hear God saying. In doing so, we listen to God through Scripture, silence and contemplation, through quiet days, retreats and meditation, through the ministry and guidance of others, through prayer and through corporate worship, which is the real 'work of God'. This kind of listening is a solid foundation on which to build a fresh expression of church.[6]

'Loving and serving' is enhanced by the posture of 'work'. There is a call to reflect God's creative activity, including practical service (however humble) for the benefit of all. This may include outdoor activities and care for the environment, charitable events and even menial tasks for the good of the wider community, as well as study and reflection on living out our faith in practice. Acting on this call means that pioneering community development work is Jesus-centred and not just heartfelt social action.

'Building community' is enhanced by the posture of 'stability'. In an age of constant change, we naturally crave an 'anchor' point in life. Society has a need for constancy, and this can be found in a stable Christian community, where we learn to live together in love even with those we find most difficult; where we inhabit the present moment and are not distracted or worried by the *'what if's'* that clamour for our attention. A pioneer community such as this will be one where deep relationships are formed, meaningful discipleship happens, and strong foundations are dug to withstand the challenges and obstacles that come along.

'Exploring faith' is enhanced by the posture of 'transformation'. In Benedictine spirituality, there is a commitment to being changed and to seeing the need for this; to seeking to realise all the potential that God has put within us; to being open to God's transforming love and grace in us; and to becoming more Christ-like. There is too a desire to seek the transformation of unjust structures in society. This kind of exploration of faith in a fresh expression will, therefore, definitely involve praying for the transforming work of God in the lives of others.

We felt that the fifth stage, of 'church taking shape', was where all four aspects of the vows would be present, as these patterns and postures of spiritual life don't stop once something has formed. They should inform its worship, discipleship and mission. The sixth stage, of 'reviewing' (or 'doing it again'), is essential if a fresh expression is to continue to respond to the world around it; again, all four vows will inform this. This process brought renewed interest and attention to this ancient tradition, and allowed it to respond to a changing missional landscape.

The old and the new then overlap and can be held together in the same expression of church or mission project, co-creating to form something fresh. The old and the new can also co-exist side by side, held as distinctive from each other, in different expressions of church or missional projects. The mixed ecology gives permission and provides a process for all of this to happen, and in doing so it increases depth and resilience.

So why do we need the mixed ecology?

There isn't one way of being church

A big question arising out of the Covid-19 pandemic was, 'What makes something church?' Some of the fundamental ecclesiological conventions were being taken away, raising concerns about how we function without them and, indeed, whether we can be who we are in their absence. Particularly pithy was the debate about whether Communion could be celebrated when the celebrant and congregation were online. Is bread and wine blessed if consecrated over the internet? We're not going to tackle that question here, but I mention it to make the point that the mixed ecology by its very nature asks similar questions. When diversity is present and convention changes, where are the boundaries? What prompts us to respond, 'Yes, this is an example of what we are aiming to do' or 'No, this is outside what we are aiming to do'? Much has already been written on what the church is, but it's important to pause here briefly to define this before we move on to explore what constitutes a mixed ecology of church. Here are three definitions I have found helpful.

First, the *Mission-Shaped Church* report defined a church as 'a group of Christians predominantly drawn from a discernible neighbourhood, culture or network, who are led by those with authorisation from the wider church, whose worship and common life includes regular commitment to preaching the word and to the celebration of the dominical sacraments'. It went on to add that this was about being 'a missionary church, one that is focused on the Trinity, incarnational, transformational, making disciples and relational'.[7]

Church, therefore, allows a trinitarian theology to shape it, through the creative provision of the Father, the transforming work of the Son and the revelation and insight of the Holy Spirit. For the mixed ecology to grow in all its biodiversity, it will need to be responsive to the world around it, genuinely open to the unknown and rooted in the 'missio Dei',[8] the work of God. As the theologian Jürgen Moltmann writes, 'It is not the church that has a mission of salvation to fulfil in the world; it is the mission of the Son and the Spirit through the Father that includes the church.'[9]

Second, Michael Moynagh offers a framework that describes the essence of church as comprising four aspects: 'with God', where God is experienced directly; 'with one another', where the church interacts relationally in worship and in discipleship; 'with the world', where the church is engaged with the outside world, and 'with the wider church', where the church is connected to other Christian communities.[10] This is helpful in thinking about a mixed ecology, as it doesn't describe one 'way' of being church, one tradition or one denomination. It could equally be about the essence of an ancient Eucharistic tradition or a resource church or church plant. Offering definitions that allow a parity of esteem is the key to developing a mixed ecology.

Third, Karen Sawrey's *Infographic Bible*, written in collaboration with biblical academics and theologians, offers amazing visual representations of data that bring huge insight and creativity to Scripture. The infographic on 'the Church and the Kingdom of God' outlines the different metaphors that are used to describe the church within Scripture and the number of times they are referenced: body (eight times); sons and daughters (five times); bride (four times); temple (four times); house (three times); pillar and fortress of truth (once).[11] Here we see themes of close relationships, of the value of people over projects, and of community. Again, for the mixed ecology to be an integrated one, different expressions of church and missional communities will need to get to know one another better, form deep relationships that cross divides and foster a radical, committed and sacrificial community of love and service.

We will draw on some of these themes in the chapters that follow. What strikes me in these three definitions, however, is that all have an element of connectivity within the church, between the church and beyond the church. This is a key ingredient of the integrated mixed ecology.

The Covid-19 lockdowns of 2020 and 2021, which precipitated the rapid closure of church buildings and limited in-person meeting, represented a sea-change moment for the churches. Some embraced the creative challenge of thinking outside the box; others experienced huge disruption that challenged their practice and worship. I remember seeing one church noticeboard with a big sign written in red ink, saying, 'This church is closed; for more information, call the vicar on ...' I think whoever posted it meant that those who might in more normal circumstances have entered couldn't go into the building, but the message seemed rather bleak and gave the impression that all activity had ceased. Were the people of God closed too? Maybe they were; I don't know! Certainly, there was criticism in the national press that churches had just shut their doors and abandoned their communities, but from my own observations this was simply not the case. Church communities across the country were engaging with and supporting their local parish populations in a multitude of ways, and with great diversity.

During this time, some church communities brought in technical equipment and turned their worship spaces into TV studios. Others propped up a smartphone to live stream from their places of worship or their homes. Many churches, when allowed, started to meet outside and rediscovered just how much this can offer. The church we were part of at that time got really creative and hosted a drive-in service in a field, where we tuned in on our car radios. It also hosted a socially distanced outdoor nativity in a school car park. What struck me in the midst of this was that there wasn't any one way of navigating these times: many local ecosystems emerged. In the church my father attends in Sussex, it was usual to have a live-streamed Sunday service, Zoomed morning prayers and WhatsApp prayer groups. And when churches were allowed to meet physically again, the hybrid church emerged, with an ecosystem of physically gathered and digital church. More broadly, large ecosystems developed where big national webinars connected like-minded people who were developing online or outdoor churches.

The pandemic prompted a need for change, and diversity flowed naturally. Churches were given permission to experiment and helped one another across the ecosystem with an acceptance that it was OK to find your own way of doing things. A few years on, I'm not sure this is the same. As the surgical masks were discarded, so was the sense of unity in diversity and the urgency of innovation. I hope these things are still there under the surface but, whatever the case, the pandemic proved that there is indeed more than one way of being church, and the mixed ecology helps both to promote and to support this. Ric Thorpe, Bishop of Islington and founder of The Gregory Centre for Church Multiplication (CCX), often says, 'To reach everyone, we need everything.' I would wholeheartedly agree.

The changing landscape of the church

As part of a job interview I attended a few years ago, I was asked to give a presentation on the challenges facing future church leaders. In preparation for this, I asked a number of friends and colleagues what they thought, and also threw the question out on social media. What came back was really interesting: 'Complexity will be the norm'; 'There will be a need to go to the edges of the church and society'; 'Enabling others will be vitally important'; 'Safety and stability will need to be replaced with creativity and innovation'; 'Be sure of your own calling'. Depending on your personality type, this may seem an exciting list or a terrifying one. Either way, it tells us something of the changing nature of the Western church.

I come from a long line of clergy on both sides of my family. They date from the 1600s on my dad's side and through to my grandfather, my uncle and contemporaries in my extended family on my mum's side. My grandfather and I were both vicar of the same church in Sydenham in South-East London, albeit seventy years apart. I was always struck by how different our experiences of this community must have been. When I arrived, the church building had been pulled down, the congregation had decreased and the civic role of the vicar had changed.

Christendom, which may be described as the primacy of the Christian world view in public affairs, is dying and the church needs to respond to this. I teach on missional ecclesiology at St Mellitus College and I sometimes ask my students how dead they think Christendom is. I count down from 10 to zero and invite them to raise their hands at the appropriate moment – 10 being fully alive and zero being well and truly dead. Most seem to average out at about 3–4, and I think I would agree; 48% of the UK population identified themselves as Christian in the 2021 census, whereas 6% are thought to be active practising Christians.[12] People still often attend a church wedding or funeral, and the British monarch is still crowned in a Christian service in Westminster Abbey. Yet most people, although open to spirituality, don't believe in an absolute God. It seems that Christendom remains alive to some extent, though bedbound and in need of regular medication.

Stuart Murray offers some helpful thoughts on why Christendom is in decline. First, the biblical narrative is increasingly unknown. This shouldn't be new territory for most of us, but I'm not always sure we know how to respond. The Talking Jesus research published in 2022 asked those beyond the church what the big questions were that they were thinking about in life. In anticipation, the researchers listed possible responses, such as, 'Is there a purpose to life?' and 'Will everything be OK?' Fascinatingly, the most popular answer was 'None of the above'

(22%), and the least popular response was 'Is there a God?' (2%).[13] In Christendom, we knew the questions and probably most of the answers; in a post-Christendom world, we need to see things from a very different perspective and from beyond the walls of the church.

Second, there is the rise of the 'unchurched', those who have never attended church, as opposed to the 'dechurched', those who used to attend but no longer do so. This shift means the idea of hosting a 'back-to-church Sunday' event just isn't going to work any more. Third, Murray makes the point that 'post' means 'after', so Christendom is still breaking up. What replaces it hasn't yet emerged. This being the case, we need to be attentive to the global, national and local 'sounds in the ground', as an acquaintance of mine from Texas would often say. Fourth, mission, community and worship are the traits of emerging and new expressions of church and are key areas to focus on. Last, Murray makes the point that with a post-Christendom church in mind, we now need missionaries *to* Christendom.[14]

Talking point

I was keen to get my conversation partners' responses to this, so I asked them, 'How does the church respond in this climate?'

Andrew: Society is changing, so we need a variety of approaches to mission and community. We are now in 'post-Christendom' and can't rely on a 'come-to-us' model, or on particular knowledge about church or faith from the unchurched in society. We need to start further back.

Beth: The church has always developed within the context she has been in. It's not that we need new forms of church, it's just that new forms are inevitable. We have a faith born out of Christ's incarnation, a faith grounded in the real and tangible experience of God expressed within creation and within human existence. As the church has grown and spread across different contexts, she has developed different ways of worship, discipleship, community and witness in these different contexts. The question is not why do we need new forms of church, but how do we together express our faith in different contexts, while remaining connected and united as the one body of Christ.[15]

Tim: If we want creativity so as to reach the diversity of our society, then we've got to let go of control of the church. In our efforts to clarify our ecclesial identity and practice, we've inadvertently excluded those who don't meet the prescribed criteria. In doing so, those who think differently, act differently and are called by God differently have left the building. For a long time, pastors and teachers have predominantly led the church, but what if we allowed the apostles, prophets and evangelists to sit in the driving seat also? These pioneering radicals might just institute the revolution that we need.

The theologian Lesslie Newbigin, typically ahead of his time, also gives some insightful reflections:

If the gospel is to challenge the public life of our society, if Christians are to occupy the 'high ground' which they vacated in the noon time of 'modernity', it will not be by forming a Christian political party, or by aggressive propaganda campaigns. Once again it has to be said that there can be no going back to the 'Constantinian' era. It will only be by movements that begin with the local congregation in which the reality of the new creation is present, known, and experienced, and from which men and women will go into every sector of public life to claim it for Christ, to unmask the illusions which have remained hidden and to expose all areas of public life to the illumination of the gospel. That will only happen as and when local congregations renounce an introverted concern for their own life, and recognise that they exist for the sake of those who are not members, as sign, instrument, and foretaste of God's redeeming grace for the whole life of society.[16]

The language of renouncing an 'introverted concern for its own life' is a harsh challenge to the church and one that is hard to face in declining institutions where a narrative of scarcity prevails. As a post-Christendom society, we are moving into apostolic times, resonant in some ways of the first-century church.

The early church was apostolic for three centuries before Constantine welcomed Christianity across the Roman Empire. The church embraces apostolic mission when it enters new territory that has not been exposed (for a significant amount of time) to the Christian gospel. This is increasingly the case in the West. Mission and evangelism in post-Christendom have to contend with decreased knowledge of Christian faith and also with increased opposition to it, because it has been rejected by society. Thinking of the parable of the sower in Matthew 13:1–23, in post-Christendom the ground is more likely to be stony, have thorns in it and be a place where birds eat the seeds of faith. Its asks more of the church as it is called to stand against the prevailing culture.

It seems the church may need to take different approaches in this post-Christendom world. Karen Sawrey again provides an excellent infographic, collating the qualities of the early Christian church within first-century apostolic culture. These qualities are especially helpful in navigating a changing missional landscape.

First, the Acts church had the DNA of 'liminality and communitas', with risk, danger and adventure creating a sense of comradeship and belonging in the community (Acts 2:42–7). Within this, mission was an organising principle, and reaching out to broader society set the shape, function and priorities of the church. (Such things may need to change in response to the context, whereas doctrine will be universal over time.)

Second is the quality of incarnational mission: the church was embedded in the missional context, which enabled it to be agile and to spread its message quickly. We might think of an incarnational 'deepening' – just as Jesus lived among us, so we as followers are embedded in community.

Third, organic systems were present that offered simple, adaptable, reproducible structures. Such 'living systems' provided a dynamic agency, and there was 'virus-like growth' where people caught the gospel message and passed it on.

Last, an APEST (apostles, prophets, evangelists, shepherds and teachers) culture was present: there were people responsible for and capable of designing and leading the mission of the church. Without these five ministries, a genuine missionary movement cannot happen.[17]

This description of the early church – a return to more organic structures, high relational values, incarnation and agility – has strong echoes within contextual missional thinking. Although a direct comparison with the Acts church is unwise, as the landscape today is very different (we are in post-Christendom; we have established Christian church structures; communities operate and function in different ways), the themes seem important and there is much to learn from them, if we are indeed entering into a new apostolic age. Yet how easy is it to grow this kind of church from within existing structured denominations? We shouldn't reject all forms of church that are dissimilar to the early Acts church, as they are still needed in the missional and ecclesiological life of the church. The mixed ecology will enable the church to pivot into the new missional landscape by holding the old and the new together. No one church can make this happen on its own – who can honestly say that they have all of the APEST ministry covered in their parish church? – and so the collegiality and shared missional agenda that the mixed ecology brings means we can be greater than the sum of our parts.

In 2018, the House of Bishops issued a statement that outlined warm support for 'planting new churches as a way of sharing in the apostolic mission by bringing more people in England to faith in Christ and participation in the life of the Church'.[18] In 2019, the Church of England's General Synod passed a motion encouraging every parish and diocese to be part of this movement; to form new disciples and new congregations to reach the unreached in their community and to aim for the creation of ten thousand new Christian communities.[19] In this apostolic climate, the mixed ecology is going to be increasingly important for the changing shape of the church.

First, with new forms of church continuing to emerge and some existing churches seeking to adapt, the mixed ecology is only going to grow and expand. By nature of being an apostolic church, a diverse ecosystem is inevitable. Second, the mixed ecology can provide a community of practice, where worshipping communities and their leaders can work things out together in this strange new world. It will bring allies for this journey, both those who are on a similar missional and ecclesiological road and those who are on a completely different one; after all, the end goal of growing healthy worshipping communities who have deep discipleship and vibrant mission will be the same, even if the outworking looks very different. Last, the mixed ecology can provide space for different expressions of church to inform and inspire one another, offering strength in numbers as the church continues to engage in a post-Christendom, post-pandemic world.

Larger denominational and smaller local mixed ecologies have been forming instinctively for many years. Larger ecosystems have emerged through the promotion and cultivation of a mix of different expressions of church, such as by central strategic funding bids supporting a whole range of different expressions of established and new forms of church. Local ecosystems have been forming out of recognising a need to extend the reach of the local church. For example, 'Knit and Natter' emerged among people who enjoyed knitting shawls and small blankets as gifts for others. A short spiritual reflection during each meeting proved popular. One member, who was coming to faith, described how she had been introduced to Trinity Church, Chester. She was involved in Trinity two days a week and Knit and Natter on one.[20] For her, church involved taking part in both types of congregation. Another, very different, example of a local ecosystem is St George's Church, Deal, which has spawned a dozen or more 'missional communities', averaging around thirty people each. Small teams gather other church members to serve a specific demographic outside the church, such as homeless people or families. These people are loved in a simple, practical way, introduced to community life, and offered the gospel if they are interested.[21]

The need for a framework for the mixed ecology of church

A framework for the mixed ecology can be helpful for a number of reasons.

It brings evidence

Research on the rise of the mixed ecology over the last decade can make a useful contribution to a developing framework. George Lings' book *Encountering 'The Day of Small Things'* revealed that the majority of fresh expressions were born out of and ran alongside time-honoured churches and that 49% of fresh expressions leaders are also leading an existing expression of church.[22] Many leaders were untrained lay people, often from inherited churches, who were instinctively starting something new.[23]

New data since the publication of *Encountering 'The Day of Small Things'* in 2017 reveals that the mixed ecology has continued to be important. The 2022 Church Army report *Paid Pioneers: From the margins to the mainstream?* assessed the journey of pioneer ministry over two decades and the relationship between contextual mission and the mainstream institutional church that has emerged. It is fair to say that this relationship has had its highs and lows, but the report highlights the way the mixed ecology has enabled mission on the margins. Many Anglican dioceses (like other denominations) have paid for pioneer ministers to go to the edges of culture and society. This support has not always been straightforward to implement: the mainstream church can set unrealistic expectations, or the long-term sustainability of projects may be in jeopardy once funding ends. Yet the fact that such funding exists has meant that new expressions of church have begun and have grown.

There is obviously work to be done in building better connectivity between the margins and the mainstream, but the report's findings highlight a number of things that are helpful in revealing the need for a framework for the mixed ecology.

First, there is evidence of a polarisation between church planting (which takes an attractional approach) and 'grass-roots' pioneering (which takes a contextual approach). The view is often held that these are mutually exclusive. The mainstream church has at times dismissed pioneering in favour of church planting. The report calls for the value of both to be seen and for the potential for one to inform the other. A framework for the mixed ecology will enable this to happen by highlighting the value of different ways of being church and what they each have to offer.

Second, the mainstream church should resist domesticating and stifling pioneers by bringing them too close to the institutional centre. A framework for mixed ecology should allow for different expressions of church and missional communities to maintain their distinctiveness and their place within the ecosystem as well as offering the opportunity to recognise and resource this difference.

Third, the report highlights the variation in methods and practice between pioneers and planters. Some will replicate and some will innovate, some will be paid and some unpaid, some are ordained and some are lay people. A framework for a mixed ecology not only allows different understandings of church and mission to co-exist, but also provides space to deep-dive into the 'microhabitats' contained within specific aspects of the mixed ecology. This not only reveals the depths and complexity of what is going on in a particular part of the ecosystem, but also brings valuable insight for the mixed ecology as a whole.[24]

There are a number of other reasons why a framework for the mixed ecology is important, and these came out of a conversation I had with the author Michael Moynagh a couple of years ago.

It brings clarification

There has been a lot of discussion about the mission-shaped church and the need for new forms of church, language that can leave church leaders bemused and confused. They already have church(es) and yet can see the need for new Christian communities. The mixed ecology provides much-needed concepts to make sense of this. The vocabulary at our disposal – planting, pioneering, fresh expressions, traditional, inherited, time-honoured – is unhelpfully fluid, as there are distinctions to be made as well as overlapping themes. There is still work to be done.

It brings affirmation

We need to celebrate the mixed ecology in all its manifestations, as it has much to offer that can be mutually beneficial. A local café church is not the poor relation of a large resource church or a pioneering missional community. Parish churches have much to offer in the ministry of life events and in serving their local community. There is overlap too in the various expressions of church: we have examples of good missional time-honoured churches and examples of good contextual fresh expressions, but we need more examples of good mixed-ecology parishes, deaneries and dioceses that have given people permission to co-grow such different expressions. Evidence reveals that being 'mixed ecological' in your thinking is becoming an important characteristic of the missiological landscape.

It brings mutuality

As the planting and pioneering movement has developed, there has been emphasis on how the time-honoured church can participate in supporting, releasing and enabling pioneers and planters. Nearly two decades on, however, the pioneer and planting communities now have much to offer the time-honoured church, helping it by offering apostolic principles, either to start something new or to do something within its existing structures.

It brings mobilisation

'Talking Jesus' (Barna, 2022) revealed that 2% of the population know a church leader, whereas 53% know someone who is a practising Christian.[25] This means that most people who have conversations about the Christian faith do so with someone they already know, and so mobilising church congregations across the mixed ecology is crucial. In a time-honoured church this might mean that those across the ecosystem who are already doing something new can encourage those who are sensing the need to do likewise. Within planting teams or pioneer communities, it might mean relying on groups of Christians to start and grow a new Christian community, groups that often come from time-honoured churches and established church plants. The mixed ecology has an important role in mobilising church leaders and lay people to think outside the box, as well as in giving them the resilience to keep going when things are tough. 'Mixed ecology ministers', the rise of whom will be explored in subsequent chapters, also need encouragement as they seek to develop new forms of church that are distinct from their parent church but often continue to share leadership, local theology and in some cases membership with one another. A framework will help people to understand and realise the potential of what is emerging.

The ecosystem framework

I love diagrams. I'm dyslexic, so I find I think best visually. For a number of years I have been exploring how to draw the mixed ecology of church. Around 2015, I was working for the Diocese of Ely as Adviser for Fresh Expressions. My job was to support the fresh expressions of church across the diocese as well as to encourage parish churches to think about starting something pioneering. As I travelled around Cambridge and the East Anglian Fens, I noticed that the new expressions of church varied in their approach. I developed the 'PI' scale to give structure to this. P stood for 'pioneer' (a contextual approach – see below) and I for 'inherited', a term used to describe expressions of church that have been passed down through congregations. (In this book, I use the phrase 'time-honoured' to describe this). After talking this through with the mission department, I began to use the following language:

- 'big P': strong presence of a pioneer approach
- 'little p': some presence of a pioneer approach
- 'big I': strong presence of an inherited approach
- little 'i': some presence of an inherited approach.

Various combinations emerged, depending on the approach and ethos of each church. A year or so later the Church Mission Society (CMS) published the *Pioneer Spectrum*,[26] which took a similar approach in seeing pioneering and planting as a sliding scale. This articulated P and I in a much better way and has been used widely since its publication. When we were using the pioneer spectrum with local parish churches, however, they would often say, 'But where are *we* on the spectrum?' This led me to think that another axis was needed so that the whole ecosystem could be represented. After I had worked through various ideas, the diagram below emerged. I've used it in lectures and workshops over the last five years and it's always fascinating to explore it.

The mixed ecology diagram

Figure 1 represents a mixed ecology of church across two axes:

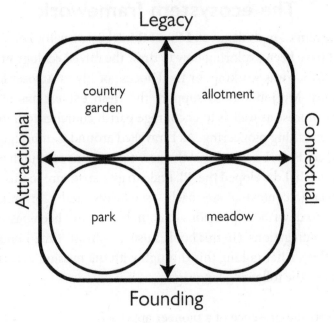

Figure 1

The vertical axis

Legacy: An established worshipping or missional presence;

Founding: A new emerging worshipping or missional presence.

The horizontal axis

Attractional: Host-led, 'worship-first' approach: worship is often the starting point, from which serving the community flows out. It is an invitational (come-and-see) approach, asking, 'Come and join in with what we are doing.' Stuart Murray refers to this as 'invitation that leads to exhortation'.[27]

Contextual: Guest-led, 'serving-first' approach: identifying the needs of the context is the starting point and church emerges out of serving the community over time. It is an incarnational (go-and-stay) approach, asking, 'What would church look like for us in this place?' Murray refers to this as incarnation that leads to explanation[28] (although I prefer exploration, as I think this is more the case in reality).

In its simplest form, four spheres emerge and different things will tend to grow in different spaces, sometimes alongside one another and sometimes apart. The analogy of different types of garden helps to explain this.

Country garden: where there are established plants and trees, dedicated flower borders, ancient hedgerows and laid-out gardens. An example of a church or missional community in this sphere could be a gathered church with an invitational approach building on established worshipping patterns and missionary activity over many years. There will often be established links with the local area, such as with schools, charities and local government or community development groups, etc. Churches will most likely be time-honoured and could be parishes, or very established church plants.

Allotment: where different plants are growing next to one another but with their own location (or row) in the allotment. Plants may be co-grown for their mutual benefit. An example of a church or missional community in this sphere could be an established local congregation who have instigated a new form of church because they realised that just doing what they were currently doing wasn't going to reach everyone, so they have responded to the surrounding context. These new forms of church or mission initiatives will exist in their own right with no expectation of people coming to church 'on a Sunday', thereby extending the reach of the parish. George Lings described these new churches as 'runners', in that, like a strawberry plant that has roots connecting individual plants, these new churches have roots in common, such as shared theology, leadership, resources and sometimes attendance (although that isn't the intention).[29] The only problem with this analogy is that, unlike runner plants, these established and new expressions of church will look very different from one another. They could be a traditional parish church that meets in its medieval building and a café church that meets in the local community centre.

Park: where there is a planned layout and defined borders with spaces that invite people to come in and enjoy features such as well-placed benches, a play area or an open space for recreation. An example of a church or missional community in this sphere could be a new church planting with an attractional approach, where a team will arrive with pre-existing ecclesial and theological expectations. These new communities may start from a place of growth, in that an existing church is now large enough to send a team to start a new plant elsewhere. They may also start from a place of decline, where an existing church has got to the point of needing revitalisation and a team plants into this to revive the worshipping community. These approaches are not mutually exclusive, of course. The planting team will very likely engage in a 'worship-first' approach as church quickly forms in a new or redundant space. Generally, these churches will start with 'something' to build on.

Meadow: where wild things are allowed to grow: self-seeding plants, different types of plant. An example of a church or a missional community in this sphere could be a very contextual fresh expression or a pioneer community. Missional initiatives in this sphere will be responding to the context around them by growing new forms of church in different places, in partnership with the local community. It could be a new expression of church that has emerged over time through listening to the community, loving and serving it, and fostering a community that prompts questions about Christian faith and eventually encourages people to say, 'What would church look like for us? – let's grow church among us here.' Generally, these expressions of church will start from 'nothing'.

These four spheres are helpful when thinking in general terms about what might exist within the mixed ecology, but in reality life is much more complex and nuanced. As I have explored this framework with students and church leaders, I have realised that almost any kind of worshipping or missional community can be plotted within it. Figure 2 gives some examples of how this might look in practice.

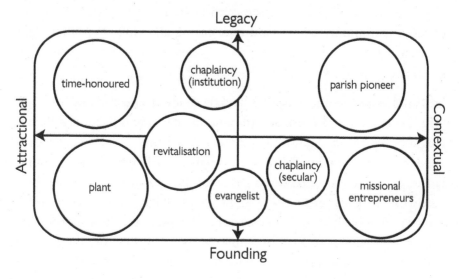

Figure 2

A theological basis for a mixed ecology

Before we explore how this ecosystem is lived out in the life of the church, it's important to underpin the reflections above with some theological foundations. Much could be said here and there is much work still to be done, but I want to highlight five themes – reconciliation, community, difference, creation and self-giving – which I think are critical for building a mixed ecology. I asked five authors to share their thoughts on these themes.

Reconciliation: Ian Mobsby

'In Christ God was reconciling the world to himself ... and entrusting the message of reconciliation to us. Therefore, we are ambassadors for Christ, God making his appeal through us' (2 Corinthians 5:19–20 ESV).

Paul's second letter to the Corinthians unpacks, for a multicultural context, the theology that lies at the heart of an understanding of

God's mission through reconciliation. Similarly, in our modern church context, each of our localities contains incredibly diverse numbers of people with different values, understandings and priorities. Paul's vision of reconciliation is cosmic and all-embracing, describing an ecclesial community where God is restoring all things back to a right relationship. This understanding of God's missional purpose is critical to any theological approach to a mixed ecology of church.

In Paul's letter to the Corinth he knew, Jews, Greeks, Romans and others spoke around fourteen different languages and lived in different neighbourhoods in a sprawling city that at the time was far bigger than Athens. Doing mission work with so many different people groups, languages and cultures required Paul and the apostles to approach their task with particular creativity. Paul needed to engage with such a mixed ecology by appealing to people's 'common humanity', showing how the love of God transcended cultural differences. We know from the anguish and passion of Paul's letters how hard it was (and continues to be now) to bring diverse people together, and how he struggled just to draw together Greek and Jew. So how do we approach our efforts to realise God's restorative purposes in order to bring very different peoples and cultures together to form expressions of mixed ecology church? For us, as for Paul, church as an expression of the kingdom of God needs to attract people beyond reluctant or intolerant co-existence into forming the new society of love, justice and inclusion. So how do we do this?

The first key theme from Paul is the idea that all Christians, all of us, are called to be 'in Christ', adopted into God's new society. We do not deserve to be 'in Christ' on our own merits, but because of the love, death, crucifixion and resurrection of Jesus. Through being reconciled, we are drawn into the visible expression of the invisible kingdom as a new society. This means in practice that there should never be one dominant culture that everyone has to conform to, but all expressions of church are called to understand that church is the coming together of people who have very little in common other than being 'in Christ'. So humility, a sense of awe and gratefulness are key starting attributes required of Christians for all expressions of mixed ecology church. Whether we are operating in a context of many different smaller missional fresh expressions of church, or whether we are part of something bigger (such as a mixed ecology parish), nevertheless a focus on unity in diversity and inclusion is an essential first step. Then the church can become a loving and hospitable place of human flourishing that celebrates diversity, rather than conforming to a dominant culture or trying to achieve unity through conformity, which can lead to power games and significant conflict.

Churches need to model this focus on humble generosity and hospitality or they will never be able to be effective missional communities responding to the diverse needs of any context. Until this kind of fundamental identity is formed, they will not be transformative. Too many churches are deeply dysfunctional and unhealthy places, with congregations who embody the danger expressed as 'hurting people hurt people', rather than what is really needed, 'transformed people transforming people'. With this emphasis on reconciling love, the mixed ecology church becomes good news to God and the world, because it can play a part in God's redemptive purposes rather than manifesting the wounds caused by the brokenness of wider society.

In addition to diversity and a common humanity, enabling a culture of reconciliation for the mixed ecology church also requires a number of other factors, including active listening, kenotic love and empathy, mutual humility, the discipline of surrender and seeing 'the other' as a gift, and, dare I say it, a commitment to contemplative forms of shared prayer.

So what do I mean by active listening? I have experienced too many churches that are really bad at this. Attentive listening really makes the effort to listen to people, allowing deep relationships of trust to form that transcend cultural divides. This type of listening aids reconciliation because it deeply humanises situations, and because it affirms people and makes them feel valued. Practising good eye contact and being willing to actively listen rather than engage in more egoic forms of talking are important skills, particularly when encountering 'un- or dechurched people', which enable them to feel welcomed rather than 'talked at'.

Kenotic love and empathy essentially convey a commitment to expressing to others the love of God that you have received in prayer, including showing empathy with those who are in distress or pain. Prayer is fundamental to living in this way.

Monk and author Thomas Merton often called the practice of humility 'the gateway' to a deeper connection with God and others and, in this context, humility allows you to step away from arguments, power play and the need to be right, and to affirm a sense of the common good.[30]

The discipline of surrender is the skill of 'letting go and letting God'. Those who are good at this spiritual discipline know that the church and mission are both God's. When individuals let go of deeply held convictions and questions that cause division, and turn to God for direction and healing, a shared reconciliation is effected, which is good for the mixed ecology church. In this way, difference, encountering strangers or people you disagree with, stops being a threat and becomes a 'gift'. Heathy expressions of the mixed ecology church will see diversity as a strength rather than as a weakness.

This leads me neatly to the important connection between missional reconciliation, God's New Commandment and contemplative prayer practices. We may recall Jesus' recitation of the Jewish Shema, which becomes the New Commandment for Christians. A clever Benedictine abbot once summarised this as 'learning to receive the love of God ... to learn to value ourselves through the love of God ... to be able to love others'.[31] This profound summary of Scripture reminds us that the mixed ecology of church is only really possible if those who take part in it are deeply immersed in the love of God, so that they learn to love themselves as a form of healing and so that they do not act out any lack of self-love dysfunctionally in their relationships, a wounding that does so much harm to church, people and mission. Our world badly needs the deeply transformative love of God, which makes reconciliation possible, and in this way resources the mixed ecology church. It is then enabled to be a visible sign of God's kingdom here on earth.

Community: Tim Lomax

The famous Rublev icon of the Trinity depicts the three holy visitors that Abraham and Sarah encountered near the great trees of Mamre (recorded in Genesis 18). It is an icon rich in meaning and theology, which illustrates the hospitality of Abraham and Sarah as well as offering insights into the communal life of the Trinity.

What we see is an expression of mutual hospitality and blessing. Abraham invites the Holy Three to stay and when they do so, both Abraham and Sarah act as generous hosts. The Holy Three, having enjoyed the hospitality provided, give an unbelievable blessing on which the future of God's saving purposes rests – a son for Abraham and Sarah.

What is happening here is that, near the entrance to Abraham's tent, at the great trees of Mamre, a community of the Trinity is established that has both temporary and eternal dimensions. Often, we feel the need to validate or defend one worshipping community to the detriment of another – as if some are legitimate and others are not – and yet here we see the creation of an impromptu and low-key community in a local context. Worshipping communities may be around for centuries or just a few months, but all have these temporary, here-and-now, and yet also eternal dimensions as they are caught up in the life of the Trinity. The missional mixed ecology celebrates and promotes this idea by seeing that all worshipping communities – new or old, formal or informal, fresh expression of church or inherited form of church, traditional or contemporary – are all an expression of the life of the Trinity, which is the only legitimising hallmark.

Flowing from the life of the Trinity and connected to the theme of community is another major concept at the heart of the mixed ecology, that of space and particularity. This is the celebration of diversity, enabling people to be other and particular, unique and distinct: in short, who they truly are. The three members of the Trinity give each other space to act on behalf of and for one another in their differences. They endorse one another's particularity and in doing so they affirm one another as they truly are.

In the life of the Trinity, unity is enhanced by a celebration of difference. This is a lesson for us. Contrary to what is often promoted in the life of the church, unity is not found in uniformity. The tremendous diversity we see in the life of the church is in fact a strength, not a weakness. It is precisely when we give each other's worshipping communities, churches, congregations, fresh expressions of church and church plants the space to be other and particular, unique and distinct, that we become more unified. When we participate in the life of the Trinity by acting on behalf of and for each other in a mixed ecology, we support the missionary activity of God in and for the world. In our mixed ecology, the way we value and support our various forms and expressions of church in our differences and uniqueness will be the key to the life and ministry of the church in a post-pandemic context.

Building on this theology of space and particularity, the mixed ecology is helping us to recapture a more holistic understanding and experience of church. If we watch one Premier League match, we only get a limited experience of the way that football can be played. But if we watch all the teams play, we can see the various technical approaches that make up the game. Similarly, it is when we survey all the forms of church within a mixed ecology that we gain a fuller insight into the question 'What is church?' The idea that any one church community (whatever tradition, style or denomination) can effectively express every element or aspect of 'church' is wildly misguided. Some forms of church are strong on the Eucharist and weak on community building; others are strong on generosity and hospitality and weak on prayer. Some are strong on mission and weak on building up the members as disciples of Christ. Others are strong on formality and weak on creativity and innovation. It's only by viewing the breadth of all the church communities that make up our mixed ecology that we gain a more complete idea of what the community of the Trinity looks like, or indeed a better picture of what it is to be community in our contexts. Because the differences we express are a demonstration of the communal life of the Trinity, the mixed ecology is something to be embraced as we see God's very life expressed in and through it.

Difference: Cathy Ross

'Diversity is the New Normal.'[32] Mission theologian Harvey Kwiyani makes this compelling argument in his book *Multicultural Kingdom*. Cultural diversity in British Christianity is the new reality of our time and is something to be celebrated. In these days of Black Lives Matter (#BLM), we have a heightened awareness of needing to deconstruct and to move beyond whiteness. Affirming diversity is not necessarily easy or straightforward, but it is certainly a biblical vision and mandate.

Feminist theologian Janet Soskice reminds us that God is love. 'We learn love through the reciprocity of our human condition, through being in relation to others who are different from ourselves …'[33] Difference is built into the biblical narrative right from the creation story. At Pentecost we see an outpouring of the Spirit so that many cultural and people groups are praising God in their mother tongue. The Jerusalem Council in Acts 15, the Peter and Cornelius story, and the experience of breaking bread and sharing wine are all powerful stories of coming together in diversity. In a unique moment in the book of Ephesians, we see Jews and Gentiles coming together. The test of their coming together was the meal table: the institution that once symbolised ethnic and cultural division now became a symbol of Christian living.[34] And, of course, we have the beautiful vision in Revelation 7:9 of all types of people worshipping before the throne.

Scottish mission historian Andrew Walls reminds us how our church today is in a similar situation to the church in Ephesus. He calls this the Ephesian moment. In Ephesus, Christians of two very different cultures could have formed two separate churches, but they did not. Christ was the peace that tore down the dividing wall between them, and they became not two distinct entities but one (Ephesians 2:14–22). It was in that very coming together that they saw and experienced what it meant to be one in Christ. Each was necessary for the other; each was required to correct and complete the other, to point out the other's blind spots. The full measure of the stature of Christ is reached only when we all come together – any one on their own is defective and deficient. There is only one church, but in Ephesus it depended on the coming together of the two prevailing cultures of that time. Today there are many cultures but the same principle still applies – each converted entity or culture is necessary for the functioning of the body of Christ in the world.

The Ephesian letter is not about cultural homogeneity; cultural diversity had already been built into the church by the decision not to enforce the Torah. It is a celebration of the union of irreconcilable entities, the breaking down of the wall of partition, brought about by Christ's death (Eph. 2:13–18). Believers from the different communities are different bricks being used for the construction of a single building – a temple where the One God would live. (Eph 2:19–22)[35]

We are experiencing an Ephesian moment today. The Christian world has greater diversity that it has ever known before, and our increased awareness of this offers us new possibilities in theology and discipleship.

We know that the Christian centre of gravity is firmly rooted in the Majority World and that we need to listen to and learn from those contexts. However, as Kwiyani has clearly explained, diversity is a reality in British Christianity too. Cultural diversity is on the rise, largely because of migration, and many of those migrants are Christians. People of African descent form 14% of London's population and 60% of its churchgoers – a striking statistic. 'British Christians prayed for revival, and when it came, they did not recognise it because it was black.'[36]

So what does this mean for a mixed ecology of church? #BLM and recent publications have alerted us again to our lack of awareness with respect to racial diversity, our institutional racism and our white fragility.[37] Perhaps this seems a harsh assessment. But diversity has many faces – cultural, racial, ethnic, gender, differently abled, age, class – to list only some. And in order to face these concerns and deal with them, we have to name them. What is important to acknowledge is that we need diversity and that it is a gift and a blessing. Our faith must cross borders; if it does not, we will stagnate and become domesticated. Research indicates that a diversity of voices will stimulate new ideas and can lead to greater creativity. 'Diversity enhances creativity. It encourages the search for novel information and perspectives, leading to better decision making and problem solving... Even simply being exposed to diversity can change the way you think.'[38] There are no easy answers to how this plays out in each of our contexts. It requires us to listen, to be generous and hospitable, to put others before ourselves and to believe that it is worth the effort to encourage and cultivate diversity in all its many forms. In these days, this really is the new normal.

Creation: Cate Williams

A healthy forest has a good mix of species. In fact, health is often measured by diversity. A forest is not a healthy one if it is just made up of mature trees with no life on the forest floor and no young trees.[39] Trees are important, but so are shrubs, low-level growth and all the invisible life that happens within the soil.

Neither is it healthy if all the mature trees are the same. Many of the creatures that are dependent for their life on a tree have a preference – a forest with only a single species of mature tree therefore can support less variety. Similarly, many creatures inhabiting the forest floor have a clear preference for certain foods.

Drawing on this metaphor, we will want to ensure that our churches offer variety – not just in terms of small and large, but in that at each level there are different species present: different large trees nurturing a variety of life within their branches, different shrubs and small plants, and different undergrowth and forest-floor ecology, not forgetting to appreciate the lichen, fungi and other less celebrated species.

Not all young trees will make it to maturity: some will lack light, or become lunch for passing deer, or not have the nutrients to thrive. But this is the way that God has modelled creation – there is an abundance of new seeds, some becoming mature plants and others contributing to the ecosystem in different ways.[40] Nothing is wasted: even those that don't become fully mature plants contribute nutrients to the ecosystem, becoming part of the soil in which other things grow or food for passing creatures.

We will want to learn to celebrate the small shoots that become part of the overall ecology, even if they never become a mature plant. The same applies to the seeds that are sown to become food for squirrels or birds rather than the plants that they have potential to become. We will also need to affirm those whose work is with these shoots and seeds, and who will never be able to celebrate a ministry that can be measured by statistics and numbers. Their work is to nurture the soil from which other plants will grow, and as such it is vital to overall health.

The overarching themes in the mixed ecology are variety and interdependence. As a forest needs large and small, bole and sapling, so we need variety within church life. Some expressions of Christian community are small and remain small, because that is their nature. Their seed is that of a honeysuckle or a Herb Robert, not an oak, and this is how they thrive. Some expressions of church life start small and are en route to becoming larger, but even the mighty oak spends many years of immaturity before achieving the size that is its potential.

Interdependence is a key theme in eco-theology: between the different participants in an ecological system, as well as between humanity and all creation. In his influential book *The Land*, Walter Brueggemann argues that when we speak of God's relationship with humanity, it should always be within a three-way relationship between God, God's people and the land.[41] God's interest in creation extends to the whole system, not just the human part. God desires a relationship with each individual sparrow, each blade of grass and lily, each human person, and longs for a community of relationship between humanity and wider creation.

The wisdom this teaches us is both a metaphor and a reflection on the interaction between humanity and the natural world. Just as interdependence between the different parts of an ecological system is vital, we too need one another. Different sizes, types and flavours of church can learn from one another, and grow best when in right relationship with the others around them.

As we move on from this metaphor, let us remind ourselves that it isn't just a metaphor but also points to a key aspect of Christian life and mission as we engage with the reality of God's world around us. We have been considering interdependence between different forms of church life, but all church life holds within it an understanding of a wider interdependence. As we need one another, so too we rely on God's creation to nurture us, most obviously in food for our bodies, but also in terms of general well-being in our response to the glory of God in creation. Mirroring this, God's creation needs us, most obviously in our response to the climate and biodiversity crisis. So this metaphor provides profound wisdom for our times and should shape our priorities as we engage together with God's world.

Self-giving: Michael Moynagh

Why does the 'mixed ecology of church' matter? The mixed ecology is a great way to become a more effective parish church. This can be illustrated by the example of Christ Church, Bayston Hill on the edge of Shrewsbury. In 2014, it was hosting a monthly Messy Church reaching young families, a weekly Tiddlywinks session for parents with under-fives, a regular Zone for young people, Stepping Out for people who enjoyed walking, Coffee in the Living Room for patients of the local medical practice, Outlook for the over-55s, and a senior citizens' lunch.

All these groups were part of the one parish church. Through them, the number of people the church was regularly in touch with more than doubled over four years to over 500.[42] The church was reaching parts of the parish it had never before connected with.

The mixed ecology of church can be conveyed through the metaphor of Holy Communion. A small group of Christians is broken off from the congregation and offered as the body of Christ to people outside the church. People gather round, receive the gift, 'consume' it, and are transformed into the body of Christ themselves. We hope and pray that they will repeat this process, and so the body is passed on to new contexts and the next generation.

The mixed ecology of church is a gift. The church has received much from the world. Just think of our buildings! Their maintenance, heating and lighting, the upkeep of roads and pavements so that people can get to church – all these (and much more) can be seen as blessings from the world. The church can respond with thanks by offering its own gifts to the world. These will include the gift of communal life with Jesus – the most precious gift the church can offer, and the heart of its life.

When you give away something precious, you make a statement about how much the recipient means to you. Just as Jesus gave his life for the world because, for him, the world really mattered, so when the church gives away the heart of its life – community with Jesus – it demonstrates how much the world matters to it. When the church offers communal life with Jesus, generosity also demands that the gift be appropriate for its recipients. If your friend were teetotal, for example, you would not give them a bottle of wine.

For some people, the gift of community with Christ will be suitable if it takes the form of an invitation to join an existing ccongregation. But for many people, such an invitation will be inappropriate. The existing congregation may be out of reach because of when, where and how it meets. In such cases, the church will offer communal life with Christ in a manner that *is* accessible – in the form of a community that meets at a time and place, in a style and with an agenda that *do* connect with the people to whom the invitation is issued. This is what is meant by contextualising the gift of community with Jesus.

Equally, however, the gift must also be appropriate to the giver. That's because gifts say something about those who give. If we give someone a tip, for instance, we are anxious to give the right amount so that we don't appear either mean or ostentatious. When a group of Christians offer communal life with Jesus, they need to ask whether the nature of the gift reflects the sort of people they are; the parish and diocese should ideally ask the same question.

This of course triggers a debate. How far should it be appropriate to the recipients? And if the expectations of the two are different, where should the balance lie? The gifts given within the mixed ecology of church involve negotiation. A balance must be struck between what fits the potential recipients and what is appropriate for those who give.

At its best, the mixed ecology of church involves the continued exchange of gifts – a Christmas every day! The new Christian community adds life – fresh energy, extra resources and new approaches – to existing expressions of church, while the latter pass on the rich inheritance of the Christian faith. So the two grow together in mutual generosity. They show the world, preoccupied with the challenge of diversity, how in practice difference can be combined with unity.

***

These five themes of reconciliation, community, difference, creation and self-giving all interconnect. We will struggle to hold to a theology of difference without first cultivating a theology of reconciliation. Likewise, holding to a theology of being broken and given away, which can seem countercultural and sacrificial, especially when there is financial and congregational scarcity, will make better sense and be more possible if we also hold to a theology of trinitarian space and particularity, where the community operates as one body. We need to see these themes as a theological ecosystem, understanding that they inform one another in an interdependent way.

Questions for discussion

1 What part of the mixed ecology do you feel most called to? Think about your passions, giftings, calling and experience.
2 In what ways can clear language and definitions help to cultivate an integrated mixed ecology?
3 How can a framework for the mixed ecology help to grow the life of the church in all its variety?
4 Where do you see some of the theological bases of the mixed ecology played out in the life of the church? Where does this need to go further?

Conversation partners

Beth Keith is Associate Vicar and Liberal Theologian at St Mark's Church, Broomhill and Broomhall in Sheffield. She is an associate tutor at St Hild and CMS/Cuddesdon, teaching courses on practical theology, spirituality and discipleship.

Andrew Dunlop is Lecturer in Context-Based Training and Pioneering at Ridley Hall, Cambridge, overseeing teaching on pioneering, church planting and contextual mission for ordinands and lay ministry students. He is researching how the mixed ecology is understood and practised in an Anglican benefice of churches.

Tim Yau is an ordained pioneer minister currently working as Interim Associate Priest in the Sprowston and North Norwich Team Ministry, in a suburb of Norwich.

Additional contributors

Ian Mobsby is Diocesan Community Missioner at the Anglican Diocese of Niagara, Canada.

Tim Lomax is Residentiary Canon and Director of Mission and Ministry in the Diocese of St Albans.

Cathy Ross leads Pioneer Leadership Training at CMS, Oxford and is a lecturer in mission at Regent's Park College, Oxford.

Cate Williams is Environmental Engagement Officer for the Diocese of Gloucester. She teaches missiology for Cuddesdon, Gloucester and Hereford, and explored various forms of pioneer ministry, including Forest Church, in her PhD.

Michael Moynagh is an internationally recognised missiologist who has been central to the development of the Fresh Expressions movement in the UK and beyond. He is also an associate tutor at Wycliffe Hall, Oxford and a senior research fellow with Career Innovation.

2

Integrating a mixed ecology

Let's begin by briefly defining an ecosystem: it is the interaction between a community of living organisms and their environment.[1] The living organisms include producers, who provide a resource (for example, grass) and consumers, who feed off producers (for example rabbits eating grass). Groups of the same or similar organisms are known as a 'population' and groups of populations are called a 'community'. The environment includes things such as water and the natural landscape.[2]

Interdependence is a key component of any ecosystem, because it is the means by which different components of the system can support one another's existence. All ecosystems will have organisms that depend on other organisms or aspects of the surrounding environment for their well-being and growth. So, if the church is to develop an integrated mixed ecology, then it's logical to suggest that this will include levels of interdependence.

Ideally, dependence is balanced and supports biodiversity. However, when there is an increase or decrease in population, this balance can be jeopardised. For example, in a simple system of grass (producer), rabbits (herbivores) and foxes (carnivores), if the grass becomes depleted it will have an adverse effect on the rabbit and fox populations further up the food chain. Or if the fox population increases, it could result in a decline of the rabbit population. In a similar way, the balance of a missional ecclesiological ecosystem will be affected by an increase or decrease in the populations of different expressions of church or missional communities. This will feel different depending on the perspective taken. Think of a deanery or group of local churches where there is a high population of one type of expression of church. Whether these are time-honoured or new Christian communities, the majority tends to set the agenda for the whole group.

Within a natural ecosystem, interdependence also means that some organisms will need to feed off others to survive. This harsh reality may be more palatable in some ecosystems than others, as it is perhaps easier to accept cows grazing on grass than foxes eating rabbits. It seems slightly unsavoury to think about an ecclesiological and missional ecosystem having 'consumers' or 'predators' that devour another organism for their survival. In this sense, when applied to the mixed ecology, the analogy breaks down somewhat. But the notion of consumers can still have a role to play in this extended metaphor.

First, some producers produce things that others can consume without destroying their whole organism. Think of squirrels eating acorns, bees consuming nectar and collecting pollen, or young animals drinking milk. In each of these cases, the by-product of the organism is consumed but it doesn't remove the organism from the ecosystem. Similarly, a product in the ecclesiological mixed ecology – time, a resource, expertise, even people – does not negatively affect the producer but does offer much to the consumer, helping them to thrive or even to exist. As in a natural ecosystem that transfers energy (food) through the food chain, so in the mixed ecology of church, energy – ideas, spirituality, prayer, missional practices, etc. – can be passed through different expressions of church, enriching each on the way.

Second, some parts of natural ecosystems will have environments or organisms that are there to absorb waste – aspects of the system that would be harmful if they were allowed to build up. In nature, wetlands – soil environments that have water on or close to the surface, such as peat bogs – act as wasteland ecosystems by absorbing carbon. A study by The Conservation Fund found that wetlands store 81 to 216 metric tons of carbon per acre, depending on their type and location.[3] Wetlands also hold back flood water, thus protecting other environments. So the idea of a wetland could be important for a mixed ecology of church. It would symbolise the ability to absorb an excess that might be harmful to the life of the church and the mixed ecology if left unchecked. Such an excess could include too many ideas for growth, too many directive leaders who want to be in charge, too many plans that aren't based on prayerful discernment. The context for such absorption – again symbolised by the wetland – could be the presence of spiritual direction, retreat centres, continued leadership development or coaching. We need to build wetlands into our ecclesiological ecosystems to ensure they remain healthy.[4]

Third, consumers play a role in maintaining the balance of an ecosystem. If a population of flies becomes dominant, spiders will help to control this by consuming them. I'm not suggesting here that if one type of church becomes over-dominant, then another should bring it down! There may be very good reasons why there will be a larger population of one expression of church and smaller populations of another. However, like natural ecosystems, ecclesiological and missiological ecosystems also need checks and balances. For example, unhealthy competition, or a culture of empire building (focusing on wealth, numbers and achievement) rather than kingdom building (where Jesus is at the heart of what is happening), may need to be reined in. In this sense, consumers could symbolise systems of good accountability, perhaps offered by a local ministry authority figure or another neighbouring mixed ecology. They could also exist within the local mixed ecology if there is a shared vision and commitment to working together and a willingness to be open to what is best for sustaining the life of the system.

This leads us to the question of whether we want to champion a system that includes 'predators' within the mixed ecology. In reality, predators and consumers are of course the same thing, but the language of the predator feels more emotive and deliberate. Within nature there are sometimes consumer/predators who don't seem to offer any obvious benefit to the ecosystem. These are organisms that don't contribute or that contribute negatively to sustaining the life of the ecosystem.

They might be invasive species, which disrupt the food chain and cause harm to native species. For example, the introduction of the Burmese python in the Florida Everglades has had a negative impact on native bird and mammal populations. Sadly, humans can be predators that adversely affect ecosystems: for example, the overfishing of sharks may lead to imbalances in the marine food chain. This is because removing top predators can result in the overpopulation of their prey species and the depletion of valuable commercial fish stocks. Humans have also disrupted ecosystems through the overhunting and poaching of endangered species such as rhinos and elephants. Pollution and habitat destruction caused by human activity can indirectly harm producers and predators.[5]

Some will see the presence of predators in the mixed ecology as 'that large church that opened up down the road that is draining the life out of the smaller ones' or 'the local institutional powers that seem to be shutting something down'. The truth of these perceptions may depend on your point of view, but it's important to highlight that not everything will have a positive impact on other organisms in the mixed ecology. Examples of predators without a positive impact in kingdom terms might be false teachers (2 Peter 2:1–3) or the devil prowling round like a roaring lion (1 Peter 5:8). We should fight against such things.

I recently preached at St Mellitus College on the parable of the workers in the vineyard (Matthew 20:1–16). This is the story of a landowner who goes out at different times of the day to find workers, but when the work is done pays everyone the same amount regardless of how long they have worked. The parable is bookended by the idea of the first being last and the last being first. I don't think Jesus is advocating a reversal of ranking in heaven where those who have been last on earth will be first in heaven, and vice versa. It is rather that if you think you will be first into heaven because of your spiritual status or what you have achieved, then you are in danger, and if you think you will be last into heaven because of your lower status or what you haven't achieved, then there is hope for you. The parable challenges our earthly understanding of cause and effect, because Jesus, as he does so often, radically flips this on its head.

Ecologists have debated whether it is a top–down (predator-controlled) or a bottom–up (producer-controlled) ecology that affects the biodiversity of an ecosystem more. The answer appears to depend on what you read. Recent research suggests that the greater impact comes from the top down, and that we should pay attention to the consumers to ensure a healthy ecosystem.[6] If this is applied to the mixed ecology of church, however, we must be careful not to show an unconscious (*or* conscious!) bias regarding what is at the top of the food chain and what is at the bottom. We should think more of the complexities of a food web rather than a food chain. Of course, the various elements in the food web are dependent on one another. But the survival of one expression of church should not be at the expense of another. Rather, the mixed ecology calls for diversity, equity and ecclesiological biodiversity, which can support a co-growing culture.

I think it can be more helpful, therefore, to define interdependence as ensuring that different ecclesiological and missional populations and communities support and benefit from one another, for the mutual benefit for the kingdom of God. This seems to be at the heart of the mixed ecology movement. A lot of smaller expressions of church and missional communities will need one another, or indeed the support of larger churches, for their survival and flourishing. Large or 'successful' churches who are self-sufficient may be unaware of their impact on other organisms in the mixed ecology – here, genuinely resourcing churches can have a positive impact. An integrated ecosystem will allow this to happen in a more planned and structured way.

For the mixed ecology to grow as an integrated community of churches, missional communities and social enterprises, there need to be some founding principles. This deeper work of interconnectedness and interdependence won't just happen on its own. There are many things that could be discussed here, but my explorations over the last few years have led me to pinpoint three founding principles that stand out as especially important.

Recognition

As I mentioned earlier, the *Mission-Shaped Church* report, published in 2004, called on the Church of England to place mission at the heart of its ecclesiology, with a greater emphasis on the missio Dei which, as Rowan Williams described it, involves 'finding out what God is doing and joining in'.[7] This gave rise to a vibrant planting, pioneering and Fresh Expressions movement. The movement is now ecumenical and international and the UK is seen as a place to learn from and partner with.

I was one of the authors of a synod report in 2019 – the fifteenth anniversary of the original report – which celebrated the growth of this burst of missional activity. It detailed the numbers of new worshipping communities and the ways in which mission and discipleship had developed, as well as calling for a mixed ecology of church. The need for increased equality in the way new initiatives and existing expressions of church were perceived – a parity of esteem – was also expressed. New expressions of church felt that they weren't taken seriously enough in ecclesiological terms, or were given a long list of criteria that they needed to meet in order to be officially established (whereas existing expressions of church didn't seem to have to do the same to justify themselves). The institution hadn't always recognised the ministry of new expressions of church. On the flip side, it had sometimes overemphasised them as the 'saviours of the church' by placing unrealistic expectations on them.

Another result of the publication of the 2019 report was the 'Save the Parish' campaign. This argued that these new initiatives were being given more focus, prominence and resources than parish churches. The term 'fresh' certainly can suggest that everything else is stale, and in some cases new expressions of church can be unhelpfully disconnected from the wider body of the organisation. Having worked for the Church of England nationally and having been part of the national steering group for new worshipping communities, I can say that this wasn't the intention. The paper set these new expressions of church within a 'mixed ecology', demonstrating that the majority of them stem from parish churches that have sought to extend their reach. I know this because I wrote that part of the paper! Whatever side of the debate you take, it's clear that there is much work to do in building a parity of esteem where different expressions of church value and affirm one another. This is hard to do in a narrative of scarcity (whether of money, roles or appointments), and it can quickly feel like the survival of the fittest. In God's economy there is always abundance, but it's easy to lose sight of this.

To build recognition, there also needs to be greater appreciation of distinctiveness. If we are to grow a parity of esteem, distinctiveness is the key, because it says, 'I know you are valued and you have a place.' Such an awareness of the differences across expressions of church and mission initiatives reminds us that 'unity is not uniformity' and that there is more than one way of doing things. This doesn't come simply by sharing information. Some of the divides are so entrenched that we will never affirm one another unless we are willing to 'experience' the other. At St Mellitus we hold to something we call 'generous orthodoxy', by which we want to recognise the breadth of different theological understandings and aspects of Christian life and faith. This is not about finding the lowest common denominator as a community, but rather about being willing to step fully into a tradition that is different from your own. I remember attending an Anglo-Catholic Eucharist at one of our residential weekends for ordinands. For some students this was very familiar territory and for others it may well have been their first encounter with this form of worship. What made it such a positive and affirming experience was that the member of staff who was presiding took about ten minutes at the start of the worship to explain what was going to happen and the theological reasoning behind the words, actions and symbols. This made the act of worship something that everyone could fully engage with. Because we did it, we got it, and more than this, because we knew the 'why', we were able to appreciate the distinctiveness even if some would prefer to do things in a different way.

Resource

The next principle of building an integrated mixed ecology is to resource one another. I am always struck by the early church in Acts and the way that it displayed an economy of radical sharing. In Acts 2, at the time of the outpouring of the Holy Spirit at Pentecost, we read of 3,000-plus believers meeting together and in verses 44 and 45 we see that they had 'everything in common' and sold their houses and possessions, sharing what they had to ensure that no one was in need. We can infer from the text that there were cultural and socioeconomic differences, but the thing that united them was their belief in Jesus through his Spirit. This is radical stuff! What would an economy of sharing look like within the mixed ecology of church? What would happen if we could really look out for one another, mastering the art of true recognition?

1 Corinthians chapter 12 is a helpful basis for exploring what a resourcing ecosystem might look like. Paul, writing to the church in Corinth, explores the theme of diversity without divisions. Corinth was diverse and multicultural, a city of a 'heterogeneous population of Greek adventurers and Roman bourgeois, with a tainting infusion of Phoenicians; this mass of Jews, ex-soldiers, philosophers, merchants, sailors, freedmen, slaves, trades-people, hucksters and agents of every form of vice … without aristocracy, without traditions and without well-established citizens'.[8] As it was set within this culture, the church in Corinth was also diverse. In verses 1–11 Paul calls for the recognition of different types of spiritual gift with the understanding that all come from the same Lord. All gifts, if they are given by the Holy Spirit, are to be used for the 'common good' (verse 7 in NIV) of the church. God's intention is for the church to be resourced and gifted by each member of the body bringing something different.

This brings us to the second part of chapter 12 (verses 12–31) and the highly applicable analogy of the body.

Talking point

Here is what my conversation partners, Janet Tanton, Craig Williams and John Valentine thought about this analogy.

Janet: The phrase 'one body, many parts' shows us the church as an organic entity. All of the things necessary for growth, survival and reproduction are in place. If everything works together, the body will not only maintain its present form but will grow and reproduce. Just like families, the 'offspring' will not be identical to the parent. While rooted to the family tree, children will live different kinds of lives from their parents.

Craig: At least two points stand out for me. First, we hear that there is variety in the expressions of church, that one size doesn't fit all. Second, it tells me that leadership in the body is dispersed, not centralised. There is one head, Christ, from whom we take our cues. But leadership needs to be dispersed from there.

John: I love this application! The more we can get away from disdain and self-denigration in the relationship between different approaches to church, the better! Equal honour could become a watchword (verses 23–26). The more we can strive to give 'greater honour' to different approaches to mission and church, the more the body of Christ as a whole might be effective. I love it when people speak well of others and other churches and approaches to mission![9]

As this famous passage sets out, Christ is the head and the people of God, the church, are the body. First, there is belonging: a foot can't say it doesn't belong because it is not a hand, nor an ear because it is not an eye. All belong and all are part of the one body (this brings us back to the idea of recognition). Second, as with Paul's discussion of spiritual gifts, not all body parts have the same function and therefore all bring something different. If we are in Christ, we are part of something infinitely bigger than our individual selves (verses 12–13). *The Message* translation puts it like this:

By means of his one Spirit, we all said good-bye to our partial and piecemeal lives. We each used to independently call our own shots, but then we entered into a large and integrated life in which *he* has the final say in everything. (This is what we proclaimed in word and action when we were baptized.) Each of us is now a part of his resurrection body, refreshed and sustained at one fountain – his Spirit – where we all come to drink. The old labels we once used to identify ourselves – labels like Jew or Greek, slave or free – are no longer useful. We need something larger, more comprehensive. (1 Corinthians 12:13, MSG)

In this way, the church can resource itself. For the mixed ecology to work, we need to think beyond our own walls, boundaries and 'body parts'.

Third, in order to be able to share the resources we have, we need to think less of ourselves. This doesn't mean that we shouldn't celebrate our giftings and resources (I think we need to do more of that!), but rather that we shouldn't think of our gift as just for our use or that it is better than someone else's. Ironically, if we hold tightly to what we have, we will be the poorer for it. There is an old Chinese parable about heaven and hell that a friend of mine used to recall. In both places there are big bowls of rice and six-foot-long chopsticks. Even though the bowls and sticks are the same, in heaven everyone is full and in hell everyone is hungry. The difference is that in heaven people are feeding one another, whereas in hell people are trying to feed themselves, but unsuccessfully; you can't get a six-foot chopstick into your own mouth. So as the body of Christ we are encouraged to work together. This speaks especially to those who feel that what they have to offer might not be as flash or as needed compared with what others may have. As we see so often in the Bible, it is in the more unexpected places that the greatest treasure can be found: jars of clay and all that!

Fourth, I am always intrigued by verse 18, stating that God has placed the parts of the body in perfect balance. The Amplified Bible (AMP) puts it this way:

> But now [as things really are], God has placed *and* arranged the parts in the body, each one of them, just as He willed *and* saw fit [with the best balance of function].

If, therefore, we sense scarcity in the church of today, then either the balance is wrong owing to poor decision making, or we're not looking closely enough at God's provision. Whatever the case may be, the key is that the mixed ecology of church should seek to resource itself not despite its differences but *because* of them.

Resilience

The third principle of growing a mixed ecology of church is a commitment to resilience. In reality, local integrated mixed ecologies are hard to build and to sustain. Research has shown that it takes 'team, time and tenacity'[10] to do this, so resilience will be a core factor in enabling this to happen. There are many examples of resilience in the natural world: think of limpets clinging to the rocks when the tide comes in and out, or penguins who brave the harsh minus-25-degree climate of Antarctica. The mixed ecology of church may not have to battle the sea and the cold, but it will need to work hard to achieve interconnectivity. How can it build its resilience to combat individualism, misunderstanding and a lack of vision?

In her book *Irrepressible*, Cathy Madavan talks about the different ways in which we can be purposefully resilient. I love her pithy chapter titles, a number of which are helpful to this discussion.[11] First, she talks about 'knowing your purpose' – what we were each put on this earth to do. If it's not clear why we are doing what we are doing then it's hard to keep going when things get tough or our circumstances change. I have been part of organisations and churches in the past that haven't had a clear mission or vision statement. In this situation, when difficult decisions or problems come along, it is harder to weather the storm and decide where you need to go. Cathy quotes Pablo Picasso, who said, 'The meaning of life is to find your gift. The purpose of life is to give it away.'[12] It is vital to identify your passions, because doing something because you are obliged to is very different from doing something because it gives you life. Out of this, we can serve those around us. Within the mixed ecology, then, knowing your purpose is the key to resilience for each individual ecclesiological and missional organism and for the system as a whole. If all the people in a community are living out their giftings, know their purpose and have a commitment to giving things away for the good of others, much like God arranging the parts of the body where they need to be, a mixed ecology of church will be stronger together – its strength will lie in its differences. Some communities may find identifying their gift harder than others. One local time-honoured church may have a clear ministry of serving the homeless community, or be excellent at identifying and sending out new leaders. For others, who either are good at a number of things or don't feel they have much to offer, it may be a case of entering into a season of prayer and discernment to help to identify their contributing gift. I do believe that all Christian communities have a gift and a purpose!

Second, Cathy writes about 'digging deep foundations'. This is crucial for holding firm. It reminds me of the parable of the wise and the foolish builders, the one building their house on the rock and the other on the sand. When the rains came, the house on the sand 'fell flat', to quote the Sunday school song that accompanied this story when I was a child. We have just moved to a new housing development, which is only half finished. It's interesting to watch the buildings progress: for ages, while the foundations are being laid, not much seems to be happening, and then suddenly the houses rise rapidly. If we rush to build upwards, we won't be building with resilience. Cathy writes about our character and convictions determining the choices we make, which will in turn determine the stability of what we build.[13] I remember my tutor at theological college talking to us about our 'spiritual basements' and getting us to see what was lurking there that could trip us up.

The same can be true for the mixed ecology. It's important to check what the foundations for the ecosystem are. A foundation of commitment to collaboration and self-giving will be stronger than suspicion and competition. Strong foundations will mean that the mixed ecology will be able to cope well with challenge and difference and will be resilient to the changes that will naturally come when expressions of church move in and out of the system. Good foundations in a mixed ecology of church will also mean stronger foundations in each individual expression of church. Sometimes this may need a little extra support to stop the ecosystem from collapsing. This is symbolised by the medieval foundations called flying buttresses that can often be found on the external walls of cathedrals. These arches, which extend from the walls to the ground, act as counter-thrusts to the weight of the walls and roof, enabling the cathedral to be built higher without collapsing. Mixed ecologies of church will benefit from some 'flying-buttress foundations', which bring support and protection. In trying to combine different approaches to church and mission, tenacity will be needed, as there will be a danger of things pulling in different directions or expanding outwards as recognition and resources grow and develop. To prevent this, it is helpful to find ways of supporting the system through the foundations of character (a recognition of difference) and conviction (a willingness to share resources). Sturdy individual and corporate foundations will mean that all are better protected when the storms come, so the house can stand firm on the rock.

Third, Cathy Madavan writes about learning to play jazz, which can be seen as a metaphor for improvisation and collaboration. She opens her chapter with this quote from Nina Simone: 'Jazz is not just music, it's a way of life, it's a way of being, a way of thinking.'[14] She goes on to note that 'the joy of jazz is that it takes the structure, the framework, the very principles of music but then gives permission to be playful and to improvise'.[15] In nature there are many examples of this, especially in the algorithms of the natural world. Fish and birds will swim and fly together in sequence, with no single organism in charge. There is an unspoken communication that is sensed, which enables them to work together for protection, to make it easier to find food and for navigational benefit. Think of a school of fish who can pivot together when a predator comes close. Improvisation and collaboration within a mixed ecology will be vital to its resilience. If a population of churches and missional communities can move and respond as one, they will not only be able to pivot and adapt as they seek to respond to external forces (e.g. a changing missional landscape, a new consumer, or shifting DNA in the ecosystem), but will also be better at supporting one another in their distinctiveness. As with a natural algorithm, there is no single leader; collaboration comes through connectivity.

A friend of ours is a professional drummer and has recently been performing in the West End production *Show Stopper!* It's an improvised musical where the audience suggests the content and performers improvise what is sung. Amazingly, the band also improvises the music live, creating songs on the spot without rehearsal. This can only be possible if you know the other musicians to such an extent that you can anticipate what they will do next. It is also important that you do not 'block' the other person. In theatre language, blocking is ignoring the cue you have been given and introducing your own choice or thought. In good improvisation, all performers are listening to one another and building on what the last person has said, sung or played. If the different expressions of church and missional communities in a mixed ecology can learn to improvise in this way, where they are anticipating one another to such an extent that they can deepen their relationships and work as one, then the ecosystem will grow in its resilience, both internally and regarding the world beyond it. One common problem with mixed ecologies is that they can be run or dominated by one or two expressions of church. This can exclude others and mean that not everyone has a place at the table for decision making and shaping the culture of the ecosystem. Improvising allows everyone to contribute, which will make the mixed ecology more resilient to factions, dominance and individualism.

Talking point

I wanted to see what my conversation partners thought about the reality of growing a mixed ecology based on the principles of recognition, resource and resilience, and asked them to comment on how easy is it for distinct forms of church to form relationships with one another.

Craig: We ought to be what God has asked of the church – a sign and foretaste of the kingdom. Yet how bland the church has become. New communities, if held up and supported by the parent congregation, could be a significant way forward in this area. There is no going back to what was, so every established congregation needs to ask what will be. New expressions not only give birth to new life, but enable the established congregation to be renewed in imagination and purpose, like a proud parent or grandparent. Participating generously – in terms of both budget and self-giving – reflects your values and allows you to change the culture of the established congregation. Do you have staff dedicated to this (resourcing with leadership)? Do you have a budget for recruiting apostolic leadership (a commitment to missional discipleship and sending)? Will you adjust your priorities to fit the missionary calling (letting go of the status quo, in the areas of budget, staffing, time and vision, so as to do something new)? This last point commits us to adapting to our present and future contexts, and to the work of the Spirit. One last point: give your best, not what is left over. This work is not an add-on; it is central to God's mission through us.

John: This feels doable to me, but it needs intentional mixing, talking up and honouring. Most models of being church seem to settle for keeping the various expressions of church apart. But different churches can be better at reaching different constituencies. A resource church could probably not reach an estate, but a more pioneer approach ('serving first') would be far more appropriate and effective. I suppose that different approaches also include different social and spiritual dynamics, so finding a shared approach for being together (without playing into unhelpful and maybe unrecognised power dynamics) is not totally straightforward. I think that is why the mixed ecology needs dedicated leadership for support and encouragement. It also needs buy-in from those in the congregational culture who give permission.

Janet: This depends on the type of church and the personnel involved. It is important at the outset to make sure that everyone is aware of what is happening and to give assurances that 'normal' church will continue. Sometimes, problems may arise over the question of space if church premises are used.

This was so helpful! So I asked them what they thought would be the benefits of being 'the body' within the mixed ecology.

Janet: We can learn from one another. We might discover something new. People will catch the vision of mission.

Craig: The benefits are like the proverb – iron sharpens iron. A study in the Nazarene Church in the US noted that when new expressions of church were started near existing churches, the established congregations grew. The mixed ecology sparks the imagination, creates a healthy existential threat (not always a bad motivation) and generally opens the eyes of each entity to other possibilities. If the established leadership is healthy, the proud parent congregation will say metaphorically, 'Do you want to see pictures of my grandchildren?'

And what are the possible tensions?

Janet: Some of the tension can be found in the use of shared spaces and resources, for example when things are not tidied away for the next group. Social norms may also vary between two groups of people, encompassing social, economic or class differences.

Craig: The tension is essentially a challenge to the mindset with which we view resources, as well as a challenge to our core theology. Do we believe in scarcity or abundance? Is there enough to go round or are we operating a zero-sum game? If our theology is one of abundance, the tension lies in whether we will lean into it. Another tension is that if the new expressions of church are wildly successful, it can threaten the perceived significance of the established congregation. This requires the leadership and organisation of the established congregation to keep getting healthier in its self-understanding and practices.[16]

The mixed ecology journey

So how might we go about implementing these three founding principles? The mixed ecology journey can help to implement recognition, resourcing and resilience through six stages, which time-honoured, planting and pioneer communities can follow together. Each stage of the journey has an analogy that brings further explanation.

Noticing: 'the pathway'

This is about being aware of other expressions of church. At the time of writing we have a hire car – our own vehicle is at the garage after an unfortunate incident with a skip. The hire car has some very clever technology. For example, it alerts you when you are too close to the central reservation; in a traffic jam it knows when there is traffic ahead and slows you down, and it also tells you when the car in front is moving away. After a couple of weeks, I realised that these gadgets have actually made me more aware of what is going on. I think that this is because when things are familiar, you notice them less. Conversely, when something is prompting you to pay attention, your awareness increases. So to what extent are other expressions of church and missional communities so familiar that we don't notice they are there? This could be the church belonging to another denomination that we walk past at the end of our road, the pioneer minister at the local church leaders' meeting, or the youth project in our community centre.

Once we have begun to notice what's around us, we need to be aware of how we interpret it. I trained as a coach a few years ago and I remember being taught the difference between listening and noticing. When we listen, we can at times do so with an agenda or an unconscious bias. But noticing without diagnosing is more about unbiased observation.[17] This is especially important for the principle of recognition in the mixed ecology. It means being aware of others and resisting the urge to make judgements and assumptions about who they are and what they do. It is about choosing to walk alongside one another through recognition. This could involve finding out what someone is doing by visiting in person, looking at their website and social media posts, or talking to someone you know who is part of that worshipping community. It is also about being aware of the leaders of other expressions of church and sharing information about what you do, as well as your values and ethos. All this won't just happen: we have to make a deliberate choice to walk together as strangers, acquaintances or friends. To do this, we need to be more alert to who else is on the road with us, just as I was with the hire car's technology.

In Luke's account of the road to Emmaus, we read about two of the disciples, Cleopas and an unnamed disciple, travelling away from Jerusalem after Jesus' death and resurrection. In this well-known passage there are a few principles that can help us. First, there is an openness to discussion. We are told that they meet Jesus on the road and it is safe to assume that the three of them agree to walk to the village of Emmaus together. We know that their conversation is about the recent events in Jerusalem and that Jesus speaks to them of the prophetic and messianic Old Testament scriptures (Luke 24:25–7). Once they reach the village, the disciples urge Jesus to stay with them, another intentional partnering. Second, Jesus is the one who reveals the truth and opens their eyes. Noticing other expressions of church and missional communities is only going to happen if we prayerfully ask Jesus to show us what is around us and to open our hearts. The breaking of the bread is the moment when they see who this fellow traveller is – it is an unmistakable reminder of the Last Supper that took place only a few days before. We need to identify the unique signs of God that are at work in others within the mixed ecology, and which can help us in our noticing. Third, even though they don't recognise Jesus on the road, we're told that 'their hearts burn within them' as Jesus talks with them and speaks of the Scriptures. This shows that the work of noticing others in the local mixed ecology is God's work. It also raises the question of how open we are to allowing our hearts to burn within us as we witness a totally different expression of church.

Offering: 'the gift'

This is about being aware of what you have and what other expressions of church might need. It has been explored above in relation to the principle of resource, but what could it look like in reality?

It might be that there is a practical need, for either money or people, or a need for accompaniment by which others who are further along on the journey can offer support and assistance. Or we might know enough about one another to be able to commit to praying across and for different expressions of church. Perhaps we can signpost people to others who can help, creating a network that supports different parts of the ecosystem. We may be tempted to give away things that are left over or that we don't need. After all, if we all gave away our best people and things, we'd be left with nothing, right? When I was a parish priest and I had got to the point where our Sunday school was finally up and running, I heard that the key leader who had been the catalyst for it was moving to a new town and therefore to a new church. It was so hard, but it was of course right that the leader should go where they were called to be. Giving them to another community actually created a space for others to step up in my own church. In God's kingdom there is a precedent for giving away the best, the first fruits. Deuteronomy 18:3–5 sets out what portion of food and grain was to be given to the Levite priests who were the ministers for the people of Israel. As the tribe of Levi weren't allotted land and therefore an inheritance, the rest of the tribes were to bring food and grain to sustain the priests, not just the leftovers but the 'first fruits'.[18]

So, supposing that we are living in a narrative of kingdom abundance, what would happen if we all sacrificially gave away our ecclesiological and missionary first fruits? We would all get something, wouldn't we? We may be giving a gift that would bless and grow the ministry of someone else (for example, time, resources, expertise). I like to think of this as missional tithing – a way of giving back to God and to his church in a way that will bless others even if it costs us. I appreciate this is a hard thing to do, but it could be as simple as lending some tables. I remember a new mission initiative in East Anglia that wanted to set up a stall in the town's weekly market. The project sold food and drinks and was a way of being a presence beyond the walls of the established church. But they needed tables and had nowhere to store them. A time-honoured expression of church heard of this and were able to lend them some tables. This small gesture really made a huge difference to the new expression of church.

Gathering: 'the tent'

The previous two stages have at their heart an awareness of the other, while the next two have an emphasis on action. This stage is about finding ways of being together and forming relationship. If we are to be 'the body' then we need to be in relationship with one another.

I am not a camper. My ethos is 'Why sit in a tent in the rain when you could be in a hotel watching Netflix?' (if you love camping, let's not dwell on that point). We recently had some friends to visit. As there were about thirty-five of them, they decided to bring their tents and campervans to a campsite just down the road. Typically, it was sunny the weeks before and after they came. But during that week, we recreated some very British scenes of being huddled in a rain-drenched tent with no mobile phone signal, trying to order enough pizza for everyone. Reflecting on this experience (yes, I went home to my warm, cosy bed each night), I was reminded how old the concept of a tent is. It is thought that they date back to 40,000 BC.[19] The first tents were made of animal bones and stretched hide, and they are of course mentioned in the Old Testament: for example Jabal (Genesis 4:20) is one of Cain's descendants and is described as the father of the herdsmen who live in tents.

Tents provide shelter where there otherwise wouldn't be any. They tend to be temporary structures used for a season before a shepherd moves on to new pasture or for a specific event (a camping trip, a village fête, for example), and can be put up where they are needed. They are often informal places where conversation can flow and where societal convention is waived. If we are to find ways of being with one another across different expressions of church, which (let's face it) is easier said than done, then the metaphor of the tent is a useful one. Shelter is often associated with safety, so these meeting places need to be safe spaces where the three principles of recognition, resource and resilience can be present. The pop-up nature of a tent creates a neutral territory, so it's less about 'inviting someone over to your church office', which can mean that others need to conform to your ways, and more about meeting on common land. All are therefore on the same footing and a parity of esteem can begin to be formed. We might also need to leave our own conversations at the door and find a shared way of meeting.

What goes on in these metaphorical tents? They can be venues for sharing stories, praying for others, building relationships, addressing misconceptions and offering a secure place to ask questions. But there is something else here too. In the Old Testament, the tent of meeting, also called the tabernacle, was the portable earthly dwelling place of God. It was a place where the priests would atone for the sins of the people, a place for repentance and for commonality. And if we stretch the canvas analogy even further, we can find themes of the incarnation here too. When it says in John 1:14 (ESV) that 'the Word became flesh and *dwelt* among us', the Greek word used for 'dwelt' is 'skenoo', which can be translated as 'tent'. The related word 'skene' is used to describe the tent of meeting when it is referred to in the New Testament.[20] So, as Jesus pitched a tent on earth and dwelt among us, there is an important call for those who inhabit a mixed ecology to do the same and dwell with one another, in person. This may involve a place to meet with the presence of God, a place to repent of dismissing and judging one another, and a place for building peace within the mixed ecology.

Connecting: 'the gate'

This is about finding ways of signposting to one another. Again, this is a call to action, which invites those within the mixed ecology to celebrate one another and to explore a deeper level of connectivity. If the tent gathering goes well and relationships are formed and deepened, it makes sense for us to want to help one another out. This is where it starts to get real! Craig Williams recalls that, some years ago, he appreciated the communication in a fresh expression of church in Central London. They listed all the Church of England congregations in their nearby communities each week. They acknowledged they were one of many and encouraged people to find the right fit for them. This attitude of assisting those we have yet to meet, rather than being competitive, is important. This means we are directing those who find us along a path that may be more suitable than the one we are currently involved in.[21]

As we have already noted, there is no 'one-size-fits-all' expression of church – different people across the mixed ecology will need different things. Helping people to find the right faith community is important for their discipleship and their ministry contribution, and a well-connected mixed ecology can provide the framework to enable this to happen. Finding common missional and discipleship entry points can be valuable for the shared life of the mixed ecology. With increased interdependence, it may be that one expression of church or missional community can be a gateway into another expression in the ecosystem. In its simplest form, a mission organisation or chaplaincy could help someone who has come to faith to connect with a local church. In its more complex form, someone in one expression of church could find their way into another with the help of both. This could be a seniors' craft church meeting on a weekday in the church hall, which might see people finding their way into the time-honoured Sunday congregation, perhaps initially via attendance at seasonal services. Or it could be through someone coming to a time-honoured church for their wedding, who for whatever reason feels more at home in the worshipping community in the local social club. This is complicated, as it can involve considering membership ('Who gets to choose who belongs where?'), scarcity ('If we don't have that many people to start with, why would we be actively choosing to direct someone somewhere else?') and identity ('But what we offer is the best, so why would another expression of church do this better than we do?'). In reality, there are stepping stones in joining a faith community, and especially in post-pandemic times multiple membership is increasingly common. But why wouldn't we want to do this? Are churches in the business of holding people hostage? If we are one body all playing our role, being part of the mixed ecology calls for more generosity and a bigger-picture perspective of how God is at work.

The passage where Jesus sends out the seventy is well used in pioneer circles: 'If those who live there are peaceful, the blessing will stand; if they are not, the blessing will return to you' (Luke 10:6, NLT). Pioneering is often about discerning whom God is calling you to hang out with, and whom it is not quite the right time to hang out with. There are resonances with 'whoever has ears to hear, let them hear' (Mark 4:9, NIV). Timing is everything in God's economy – it's about knowing what we need to do at what point in time. Being a gateway is about asking how each expression of church and missional community might be an entry point or stepping stone, so that someone can find what they need at that particular time, even if it is to be found in another part of the mixed ecology.

Collaborating: 'the salad'

This is about the active outworking of collaboration across different expressions of church. Each expression is distinctive but also part of the whole, and each is dependent on the other for mutual kingdom flourishing.

I have used various metaphors in my teaching on the mixed ecology over the past ten years: some have worked and some have not! For example, the use of the term 'the blended church' for a while in the 2010s was problematic as it suggests that everything is pulsed together in a blender and has lost all shape and its original identity (not great). The metaphor that has had the best impact, however, is that of the fruit salad. Think of a fruit stall, where there are lots of different fruits but all in their separate boxes. I make the point that you might love apples so much that that's all you want to eat. If that's what floats your boat, fine, but by mixing it with other fruits you can actually bring out the richness of the apple's flavour and in the process possibly discover that you like other fruits as well. The metaphor of the fruit salad is helpful because it allows each piece of fruit to remain identifiable even when combined with others. Teaching this metaphor worked best in the pandemic. We were of course all at home and on our screens, which in this case was a good thing, as I realised we could all make fruit salads live in class from the comfort of our own kitchens! What was fascinating was that each fruit salad was unique. People had different-sized bowls and knives, had chosen different fruits (often according to their taste preference), had used different quantities and had cut them into different shapes and sizes. Once we had made the fruit salads, we would 'show and tell' on screen and the variation was there for all to see.

My mother-in-law, Helen, is an amazing cook! She lives next door to us and cooks us delicious cakes and restaurant-quality meals! She has a library room in her house that is full of shelves holding 663 cookery books and counting! One that is especially fascinating is *The Flavour Thesaurus*.[22] It's a book that lists flavour combinations, setting out which flavours pair best with one another. Some are fairly obvious, such as pork and apple, or mint and potato. But some are very surprising, for example cucumber and rhubarb, or banana and chicken. But what's also important is that some flavours just don't go with one another: no one would want to eat sausages and custard! Applying this to the integrated mixed ecology, it is clear that some combinations will be obvious and some less so. The reality is that some won't work as well as others, and that's OK.

When applying the analogy of flavours, it is perhaps best to think of a whole meal, where we might eat all kinds of flavours over two or three courses but wouldn't eat everything at the same time. With this in mind, I believe there are many types of mixed ecosystem, including systems within systems. All will be different depending on the local context, the people involved, the needs that are being addressed and the calling of each expression of church. So in this sense the mixed ecology is a fruit salad made of lots of smaller fruit salads. In the research on, and the lived experiences of, the mixed ecology that I have been involved with, I've noticed that ecologies are often of different sizes. Some will be very small, a micro system: for example, a local church community where there is an established gathered church, and a parallel fresh expression with small mission-focused activities. Some will be medium-sized, a medio system: for example, a local town or village where there are a mix of different expressions of church, some established and some new, as well as a mix of denominations and traditions. Some will be much larger, a macro system: for example, an Anglican diocese or a city, or churches within an ecumenical movement. The fact that the mixed ecology is made up of this complex network of systems allows for the different flavour combinations to exist in the way that is most beneficial. Integration begins to form out of noticing, giving, gathering and connecting, and in reality brings a much bigger story to life, as different expressions of church exist in active relationship with one another, championing and supporting one another.

When I was in South America on my gap year, I worked as part of a team at a school for the deaf with the mission agency Latin Link. They taught me Galatians 5:22–3 – on the fruit of the Spirit – in American Sign Language (ASL). The lady who taught it was a Texan missionary, which means I will always hear these words in my head spoken in a wonderful southern drawl, y'all. But it always bugs me that people refer to them as the 'fruits' of the Spirit (plural) when the Greek says 'fruit' (singular). This is important, as the fruit comes as a unit, like a bunch of grapes; so, unlike the gifts of the Spirit in 1 Corinthians 12, which are plural and are given to different people, the fruit will be a natural result of the work of the Spirit living in us. More than that: the different aspects of the fruit will surely help one another. Kindness isn't always easy and may need a dose of patience, or love may need to be mixed with gentleness to be received well. So, as the fruit of the Spirit works together, different ways of being church will start to collaborate with and inform one another: a church that is strong in discipling its congregation may help another that is more experienced in mission, and vice versa. Churches and missional communities may combine to support one another in shared leadership training or community social action projects. And a collaborative ecosystem will only truly be able to work together if the fruit of the Spirit is embodied by its leaders and worshippers.

Co-creating: 'the bee'

This is about actively working out the growth of different expressions of church through cross-pollination. As a bee by moving from one plant to another pollinates the plants, so those working in the mixed ecology can collaborate by actively working together to create something new. Co-creating is the ultimate expression of the mixed ecology of church. Rather than seeking to support one another through collaboration, co-creating is about different expressions of church working to grow something new together. This co-growing involves a shared vision and a commitment to working together, a desire to hold to shared values and defined roles, and a sense of being able to allow things to unfold even if they look different from what is anticipated. This has been happening for many years in the Messy Church movement, where churches of different denominations have worked together to start a new expression to serve their local area. Conversely, a bad example of this was in a deanery in a diocese where the churches decided to club together to fund a youth worker. This role was to involve working on behalf of all of the churches to connect with young people in the local area and form a new expression of church. The problem came when young people did start to appear, but not in the churches that had supported the youth-worker post. There were perhaps some misconceptions and miscommunications about the aims and expectations, but some within the deanery found it hard to accept that young people were being reached but weren't coming to their existing churches.

I love the account of the feeding of the 5,000 in Matthew 14:13–21. It's a story of amazing co-creating. You'll know the story well, I'm sure: a crowd is following Jesus, evening falls in a remote place, and they are hungry. Jesus, using five loaves and two fish, performs a multiplication miracle and all are fed. There are some wonderful themes in the text that reveal what good co-creating looks like.

First, Jesus responds to the context around him by listening as the disciples insist that the people are hungry and need to go and find food. Jesus could have agreed, but instead says that they need not go away and asks the disciples to provide something to eat (verse 16, NIV). Good co-creation is about responding to the context around you, seeing what might be possible locally and using your initiative.

Second, Jesus uses what is at hand and gets everyone involved. He asks if anyone has any food and the fish and bread are brought forward, not by the disciples but by one of the crowd. I like this, as the food needed for the miracle to happen comes from the very people Jesus is seeking to help. Contextual mission is all about this: rather than Christians coming to do something for, or (worst case) to, the local missional context, it's about 'being with' the local community and working in partnership. Sam Wells has written on the idea of 'being with': it means promoting direct interaction that puts the person/s at the heart of the story, and cherishing assets first (bread and fish!). He writes, '"Being with" seeks to model the goal of all relationships: it sees problem solving as a means to a perpetually deferred end, and instead tries to live that end, enjoying people for their own sake.'[23]

Third, it's not immediately obvious what Jesus is going to do. The food-to-people ratio is very unbalanced and yet the miracle unfolds in front of them. In the end, everyone has their part to play: the crowd, the disciples and of course Jesus, who enables this miracle to happen. Co-creation may not be an obvious process. Sometimes what emerges might look different from what we thought was going to happen. So for co-creation to take place in the mixed ecology it needs to use what is at hand, be open to working with those in the local context, and expect the unexpected. If this happens, many wonderful ecclesiological and missional communities will emerge that might not otherwise have existed.

So what form does this journey take? These six stages can be approached in two ways, as a cumulative journey and as a simultaneous journey.

A cumulative journey (Figure 3) is a six-stage process in which different expressions of church and missional communities engage with one stage at a time, starting from noticing and working their way through to co-creating, each building on the previous stage. You can't gather or connect if you don't know who else is there. It makes sense too that for different expressions of church to help one another to co-create, connectivity and integration might need to be present. In reality, the specific vision and agenda of an expression of church may mean that it will not always get to the co-creating stage, but I would think that at least aiming for connectivity would be enough to grow an integrated mixed ecology. This process may take months or years, depending on the ecosystem, the intention and the context.

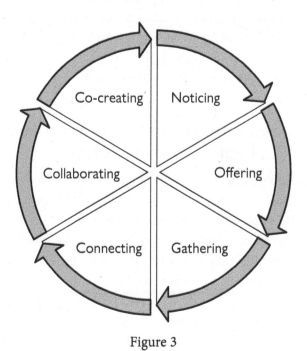

Figure 3

A simultaneous journey (Figure 4) is where all six stages are in play at the same time. At any point, different expressions of church may engage with any or all of them. In reality, this is likely to be a more common approach, as life isn't divided into nice neat stages. It is also the case that these stages will inform one another and promote mutual growth.

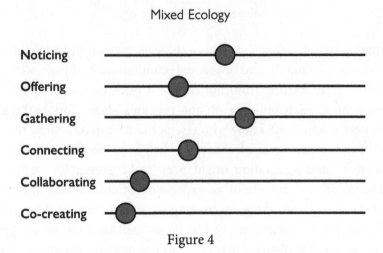

Figure 4

For example, the stage of 'gathering' may help you to further 'notice' what's around you. Again, this all takes time and, as the process is more integrated, it may be harder to measure which stage is at work and to what extent. It might be helpful to look for the emergence of recognition, resourcing and resilience as markers of progress.

What does the integrated mixed ecology look like in practice?

Once the founding principles have begun to be established and the stages of the mixed ecology journey are engaged with, connectivity will begin to form. Again, while on my travels as a diocesan adviser in the wilds of East Anglia and then in my work for the national Church of England, I began to notice the different ways in which churches were working together. I describe these as 'footprints', in the sense of the 'footprint' of a house that defines the overall shape and purpose of the building. Each footprint is made up three elements: *people*, a hub where people gather; *pathways*, the route and flow of activity; and *process*, the flow of worship, evangelism and discipleship. As I continued to observe, I found lots of different repeating footprints. Here are the four that I think are most common. They can be used to describe the way different expressions of church interconnect and how an ecclesiological ecosystem might operate.

Parallel: Two things happening at the same time (Figure 5).

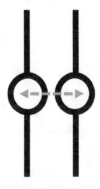

Figure 5

This is where different expressions of church or missional communities co-exist and there is an exchange or movement between them. They may be worshipping in the same premises or in the same geographical area. Both are distinct and are aware that some people may attend both, opting in and out. Both are prayerfully and practically supporting the other.

Progression: Two events happening at different times and places, where one leads into another (Figure 6).

Figure 6

One expression of church or missional community acts as a gateway into the other through mutual agreement. It could be that one acts as a natural or intentional stepping stone for the other.

Partnership: Working in partnership to create something new, forming a hub (Figure 7).

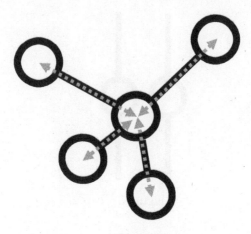

Figure 7

Different expressions of church or missional communities are supported by a variety of resource partners. This could be practical, with shared leadership or a local priest leading the sacramental aspects of worship in a lay-led church.

Precursor: What happens before or in preparation for an event could also become church (Figure 8).

Figure 8

Different expressions of church or missional communities make a commitment to meet to plan a community event. As a result, social and missional growth happens. But as people continue to plan and draw others into the planning, relationships form that can be more significant than the community project itself.

Here is a worked example showing how all four footprints could work together (Figure 9).

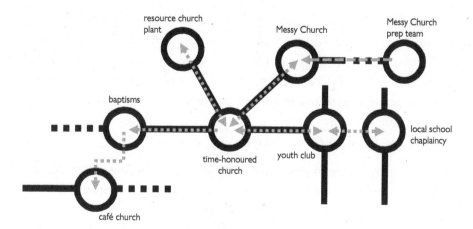

Figure 9

Parallel: The time-honoured church has a youth-church congregation as part of its ministry. The local secondary school has an active chaplaincy team. These two ministries sit side by side, with students from the school attending the youth church as well as chaplaincy meetings in school. They may invite school friends to the youth church.

Progression: The time-honoured church conducts regular baptisms. Some families are already members of the time-honoured church; others are not part of the church. Some of the new families settle in the time-honoured church; others don't but are invited to attend the café church that has been started by members of the time-honoured church who have identified a need for a different tradition of worship.

Partnership: The ecumenical Messy Church that meets in the village hall is in relationship with other local expressions of church. The time-honoured church supports the Messy Church with resources, and in return the Messy Church team have been working with church volunteers who run the Sunday school and all-age worship to give them ideas and support. The resource church that has been planted locally is also in partnership with the time-honoured church and has been mentoring church home-group members. It is also running an Alpha course across the two expressions of church.

Precursor: The Messy Church is in need of help to prepare for each session, involving cutting out shapes, making up table resource bags, and so on. Through the local Churches Together hub, it has asked for volunteers from different expressions of church to come and help. This has actually resulted in some Christian and non-Christian people meeting. In working with the Messy Church team, discipleship is emerging as the themes are discussed.

By committing to the principles of recognition, resourcing and resilience, and by choosing to work through the six stages of the mixed ecology journey, these different footprints will start to emerge. As they do, and as the mixed ecology starts to form, more foundations will gradually be revealed. Mapping these can be very useful both in identifying what is happening and in being more intentional about how to support the continued growth of the mixed ecology.

Questions for discussion

1 How easy is it to recognise other expressions of church within the mixed ecology if they are fundamentally different in their approach?
2 To what extent does reconciliation need to happen in order to start to integrate a mixed ecology?
3 Where have you seen the various stages in the mixed ecology journey at play? How could these six stages be cultivated further?
4 In what ways could you capture the foundational footprints that may already exist within your local mixed ecology?

Conversation partners

Janet Tanton is a Licensed Lay Minister in a rural benefice in West Norfolk. She leads a team in outreach and pastoral care to the small rural village where she lives.

Craig Williams is a pastor, coach and author based in California, USA and has worked in the arena of fresh expressions of church for over twenty-five years.

John Valentine is Dean of Local Ministry Programme, Diocese of Guildford.

3

Inhabiting

I love the BBC TV programme *Race Across the World*. Contestants have to travel overland from one part of the world to another, using only the price of the equivalent plane ticket. Working in pairs, they have to race thousands of miles through five checkpoints, using trains and buses and at times hitchhiking. By taking the overland route through towns, villages and wilderness, they experience so much more of the journey than if they had travelled by plane, and the eventual destination makes more sense to them. The contestant pairs are often husband and wife, parent and child, or childhood friends, and it's heartening to watch their relationships deepen as they travel. In some cases contestants actually don't mind if they haven't won, as the experience has been the most important thing. It proves the old adage that 'the journey is more important than the destination'.

On my South American travels I was lucky to be able to visit Machu Picchu in Peru, a fifteenth-century Inca city balanced on a 2,430-metre mountain ridge, often referred to as the 'Lost City of the Incas'. I have actually been twice – a couple of years apart. The first time I went, I did the Inca Trail, a three-day hike through the foothills, camping en route. At times the trek is easy going and at times more challenging. On the final morning there is a short walk before you enter through the Sun Gate and descend into the city below. It's an amazing moment as the stone gate perfectly frames the city, and it's a welcome reward for all the walking and camping (you'll recall that I'm not a camper). The second time I visited, we went by train on a three-hour journey from a busy station at Cusco in the foothills, ending at an even busier station higher up at Machu Picchu, where there are shops, people selling souvenirs on the streets and lots of other day trippers.

I remember feeling really underwhelmed the second time around. It wasn't because I had already been there, it was because the journey was so different. The train scooped you up from one place and dropped you off in another. The landscape did change as we looked out of the window but we missed a lot as we chatted, tried to find our cameras, looked at the map, and so on. In contrast, hiking the Inca Trail allowed me to inhabit the journey. By walking I was more attentive to the landscape and the people around me. The environment changed as we climbed higher. I felt that I remembered every one of the many steps that were carved into the hills, especially when the going was tough. The final destination of the Sun Gate seemed more real as it flowed out of inhabiting not only the physical place but also the journey that so many people had made before.

Given how fast-paced our lives are, I wonder how often we are really inhabiting the places and spaces in which we live, work and worship. It's easy not to live in the present, instead always thinking analytically of the past and pre-emptively of the future. We end up missing what is going on in front of us and can begin to detach from the world we are inhabiting. Within the mixed ecology of church there will be many and varied habitats – the places and spaces of different expressions of church and missional communities and the contexts in which they exist. Being clear about what constitutes these habitats and how they can best be inhabited will be the key to the growth of an integrated ecosystem. If we don't do this work as individual communities first, it will be harder to grow a vibrant and connected mixed ecology. It's a bit like the aeroplane safety announcement where, if you are travelling with children or dependants, you are told to put your own oxygen mask on first before helping them. This can feel counterintuitive – parents or carers will instinctively want to put others first – but there is logic in that if the carer isn't in a place of stability, they can't help others. Expressions of church that are healthy in the first place will grow a healthy mixed ecology.

Habitat

I once had a really embarrassing conversation with a friend whom I hadn't seen for a while. They had started working for Habitat, so I quickly launched into what I liked about this season's homeware design and asked what their thoughts were on the company's new online and supermarket subsidiary business models. As the conversation continued, it took me a while to realise that they were in fact working for Habitat for Humanity, a non-profit organisation that helps families build and improve places to call home across the world. It's a mistake you make only once. They are two totally distinct organisations that are actually both connected to the notion of home and dwelling, albeit in very different ways.

A habitat in ecological terms is the 'home' of an organism. For the habitat to be conducive to the survival of the organism, there will need to be the appropriate space, food, water and shelter.[1] The presence of the organisms in the environment of their habitat, and how they engage with that environment, is said to be their 'inhabiting'.

Thinking about this as it relates to an ecclesiological habitat, 'food' may be spiritual nourishment, 'water' the living presence of the Spirit of God, and 'shelter' the notion of a church being a place of protection and salvation. Space, however, is more intriguing and worth further exploration.

The *National Geographic* writes that:

> The amount of space an organism needs to thrive varies widely from species to species. For example, the common carpenter ant needs only a few square inches for an entire colony to develop tunnels, find food, and complete all the activities it needs to survive. In contrast, cougars are very solitary, territorial animals that need a large amount of space. Cougars can cover 455 square kilometres (175 square miles) of land to hunt and find a mate. A cougar could not survive in the same amount of space that a carpenter ant needs.[2]

So what space does a church or missional community need? An obvious starting point would be to think of this in terms of a community's physical space. Christian communities will meet in a whole host of different spaces, either by default (because that's what is available or it is where they have always met), or by intention (because the space is an important part of their identity and purpose). For example, a Forest Church will want to meet outdoors, ideally in a forest or woodland area.

When I was an incumbent in South-East London, I was vicar of two very different churches. Holy Trinity met in what had been the church hall, because the Victorian church building had been demolished owing to subsidence. St Augustine's met in a Victorian church that was at the top of a hill within a beautiful nature reserve, with panoramic views of London, incidentally also with subsidence problems, but still standing. For both congregations, the buildings' space (their physical shape) and their place (where they were located) played an important part in their story, identity and practices. Let us delve into this in a little more detail.

Space and place

Holy Trinity was of an evangelical tradition and the flexibility of its building allowed for this. Its worship was informal and varied, with participation from the congregation. It saw mission as something that was at the heart of its worship, and as a result the same physical space that was used for Sunday worship was also used for toddler groups, drop-ins and community initiatives. The church building was at the end of a small driveway tucked away in a residential street, which made it hard to find, and as a result people would rarely step in off the street. This meant that it was known and present through its community relationships and engagement rather than its building, and this had an impact on its sense of place.

St Augustine's had a central Eucharistic church tradition and the building lent itself to greater formality. Its worship was more structured and liturgical, and its high ceilings, stained glass and pillars echoed this within the architectural space. As it was set in a beautiful location, there were a good number of people wanting to be married and have their children baptised there, drawn to the church because it 'looked like a church'. When we needed to raise a fairly large amount of money to fund some necessary building work, people in the local community gave generously because they recognised it as 'their local church', even though they didn't necessarily attend. This was because of the building and its place within the geography of the community.

Sacred spaces

So what are the components of ecclesial habitats or 'sacred spaces'? In his book *Seven Sacred Spaces*,[3] George Lings outlines and explores the seven spaces in a monastic community and argues that, as a church, we have lost our engagement with the majority of them. Here is a brief summary of each:

Cell: a space for being alone in contemplation, for confronting the self, inner reflection and honesty. It is a place to wrestle and puzzle, a place for renewal, growth and individual discovery.

Chapel: a space for corporate, public and purposeful togetherness, where the whole community gathers. It is hosted by leaders who issue an invitation. It is unifying, organised and planned, and pulls together elements from other places and spaces.

Chapter: a space where consensual decisions are made through debate, speaking and listening. There is corporate discussion, intentional accountability, mutual respect and a sharing of wisdom. It is a space where tensions are held in a constructive way.

Cloister: a space where both planned and spontaneous social and informal meetings can happen in a small group and through one-to-one encounters. It is a 'joining space' connecting other places and spaces, offering protection and shelter. It is a space for relationships to be formed, nurtured and resolved. It also a space for taking stock and 'changing gear'.

Garden: a space for work, purpose, productivity and resourcing. It is a space for provision, creativity, co-creation and fruitfulness, the output and produce of which are for the use and service of others.

Refectory: a space for work, rest and play – the heart of the community. This is a space for food and hospitality for both resident and guest. It provides nourishment, warmth, relational opportunity, conversation and storytelling. There is an ethos of 'service by all for all' and of 'hearth, heart and home'.

Library: sometimes called the scriptorium, this is a space for study and for the passing on of knowledge through discovery, research and analysis. It can be a place for creative expression to bless others and to pass on stories. It is a space to ponder, reflect and slow down, bringing transformation to the head and heart.

Lings argues that, too often, understanding of and engagement with the church are reduced to corporate worship (the sacred space of chapel), when in fact church is much more than this. Identifying these seven characteristic elements that have been part of Christian communities for centuries can enable a richer expression of discipleship, mission and community for today.[4]

What these seven spaces represent can be applied in a number of ways to help define the habitats that exist within a mixed ecology. First, if we identify which of the sacred spaces are present and which are absent, we are able to describe the current shape or habitat of a Christian community. Most of our current models of church revolve around chapel, with the satellites of cell (home groups), chapter (PCCs) and refectory (church suppers). New Christian communities and Christian introductory courses will probably have refectory at their core, where people meet over food to build community by means of fellowship and discussion. Different church traditions will also emphasise different spaces: for example, a strong teaching tradition will place an emphasis on library. This process of identification also helps us to see what needs to be encouraged in order to grow into a more multidimensional expression of church.

How do these seven spaces relate to the two South London habitats we explored above? The habitat of Holy Trinity Church could be described as chapel (Sunday worship), cell (strong emphasis on home groups and prayer), chapter (staff meeting, PCC), refectory (always lots of food at church and community events), library (a strong teaching tradition, running of Christian basics courses), and garden (programmes to serve the local community, such as Christians Against Poverty debt counselling courses, or parenting support at toddler groups). Cloister was less present owing to its location, which made it harder for informal and spontaneous encounters to take place.

In a similar way the habitat of St Augustine's was made up of chapel, chapter and refectory, perhaps with a different emphasis on cell in that we didn't have home groups as such but were a community that valued private prayer. Cloister was present, as the church was open for most of the day and walkers, joggers or visitors to the nature reserve would frequently drop in to 'take a look'. Garden was present in the many events, concerts and performances that took place in the church building. These events didn't have a tangible output, such as debt counselling, but did have a big impact on the work of community cohesion and well-being. For example, we hosted an annual professional pantomime where local performers would put on a production for the community in the church space (chancel steps and pews make a great theatre space!). This would attract audiences of 1,500 people each year and to date has raised over £60,000 for local charities.

Second, these sacred spaces can be used to map the habitat of the local missional context, the spaces and places in which Christian communities reside. I've used this with church leaders and students as an effective way of helping them to think more deeply about the places they are rooted in. For example, in my South-East London parishes the habitat of the local community could be described in the following way.

When I lived there, the area was going through a period of gentrification and saw lots of artsy cafés, cool urban pubs and pop-up restaurants opening; refectory therefore was part of the local habitat. Green spaces, parks, museums, the new refurbished leisure centre and even public transport were locations for people to meet and bump into one another (London, even though it is a huge city with millions of people, is actually made up of a series of villages), and as a result cloister was part of the local habitat. Chapel could be the local cinema, chapter the many residents' and society groups that sought to make decisions on aspects of local life. There was a vibrant creative hub that would seek to plan and deliver wonderful community days and art trails. Cell may well have been represented by time on smartphones and digital devices, the lone person on a park bench or the late-night commuter.

We have seen that the seven sacred spaces can describe both the habitat of the local church and the habitat of the local community. Much like the grapes of the fruit of the Spirit, they don't exist in isolation – they work together and inform each other. The challenge for the local expression of church and missional community is to see how the habitat of their Christian community maps with the habitat of their local community context. I have visited some churches and projects where these two habitats seemed to be at odds with each other. From a missional–ecclesiological perspective, I would argue that if we want the church to respond to the emerging apostolic 'post-Christian' age, we will first need to properly examine the habitats of our local communities and then build Jesus-shaped space, food, water and shelter that resonate with and within these habitats.

For the mixed ecology of church to flourish as an integrated ecosystem, there is value in being aware of the habitats that are within it. The more each expression of church and missional community can articulate and inhabit its own space and place, the more the whole ecosystem will be able to identify the similarities and differences that co-exist within it. By identifying the commonality of sacred spaces across an ecosystem, such as chapel or cell (which might be found in most communities even if expressed in varying ways), the three principles of recognition, resourcing and resilience and the mixed ecology journey will start to develop. The seven sacred spaces can therefore be used in conjunction with the footprints that were explored in chapter 2. Together, they will begin to create a detailed portrait of the ecclesial and missiological habitats of the ecosystem.

There will also be value in mapping the habitats that exist in the local community of the ecosystem. Again, this may reveal difference and commonality across the local area, which will be useful in identifying similar missional opportunities where people can learn from one another and generate the opportunity to co-create together. For example, if refectory is important in the habitats of a local community ecosystem, there may be ways in which local expressions of church can work together to think about how they can share insights or foster a joint mission project. Noting differences across community habitats will be important in identifying what is distinctive about the mixed ecology. Therefore, by identifying the habitats of different expressions of church and missional projects, as well as the habitats of the local context, greater depth, understanding and connectivity can be found.

Talking point

Here is what my conversation partners, Graham Tomlin, Terri Elton and Ian Adams thought about the importance of inhabiting place.

Graham: The pandemic revealed again the importance of place, as we were restricted to our homes, walked the streets only in the locality where we lived, and were unable to travel to any great extent. The Anglican parish system gives us a strong commitment to place, which can never be lost even in the mixed ecology. It tells us the church is rooted in particular places and communities and needs to show long-term commitment to those places and communities. A commitment to place over a long period of time allows for a nuanced and wise rooting of the gospel in both the human and the non-human environment. If the gospel is to have its transformative effect, it needs to have an impact not just on individuals but on the natural and built environment, which plays out in the quality of local relationships, the kind of housing people live in, the degree of fairness in the allocation of resources, and so on. This can only really be worked out on a local basis, community by community, which is why churches need that connection with place to enable fruitful ministry to grow.

Terri: We cannot be 'from nowhere', but we can choose *not* to inhabit the place we are in. In my lifetime, I have inhabited various places – places radically different from one another. Sometimes I was 'an insider' in that place; at other times I was 'an alien'. Both ways of being have blind spots and are gifts. The more I embrace the place I am in (geographically as well as culturally), the more I will learn and the more fruitful a partner I will be (whether in ministry or in some other form of mission). Expressed differently, not recognising and inhabiting one's place is a sure path to long-term failure. Relationships and ministry cannot take root without inhabiting place.

Ian: Each place – your place, my place – has its own story, needs and gifts. Each church needs to seek to provide a glimpse of the heavenly city in its own context – and thus shaped by and for its own context. To enable that to happen, we need to inhabit a place, giving it deep and loving attention.[5]

Inhabiting

The idea of inhabiting, which we will explore next, builds on this concept of habitat. In the natural world, 'inhabiting' is the way an organism dwells within its designated space and place. It denotes the activity that is conducted in the habitat; in its simplest form: eating, sleeping and reproducing. In ecclesiological terms, this will be the way each Christian community dwells in the sacred spaces that make up their ecclesial habitat. This means 'being' fully in the presence and purposes of God and in the people and places of the world around us. Yet it is all too easy to find ourselves in a position of doing rather than being, where activity and activism become our identity and practice. This is a risky situation, as it brings the danger of burnout, superficiality and – most importantly – leaving God out of the picture. Not all of our good ideas are *God* ideas. If we are to build greater connectivity in an integrated mixed ecology, we first need to truly inhabit where we find ourselves. Only then can we begin to identify how we inhabit this together across different expressions of church.

I wrote an article for CMS's *Anvil* journal a few years ago, exploring what I termed 'contextual inhabitation'.[6] My aim was to set out how pioneers involved in contextual mission might think about the 'starting points' and 'dwelling patterns' that make up the ways they inhabit the missional landscape:

> The major distinction that identifies the work of a pioneer is the 'where': a contextual, 'go to' approach, with the intention of growing new forms of church in that space. This is achieved by engaging in a community in such a way as to be fully present among the people and the purpose of that place where pioneers are integrated, accepted and known: the journey of 'contextual inhabitation'.[7]

Our focus here is of course wider than pioneer ministry, but the idea of contextual inhabitation can be useful in exploring the intricacies of inhabiting the mixed ecology. Therefore, we are interested in whole Christian communities rather than the dynamics of an individual leader. What are the various communities' starting points and dwelling patterns, and what difference could these make to the connectivity of an integrated mixed ecology?

Starting points

Starting points refer to how familiar an expression of church is. Expressions of church and missional communities may be made up of 'Incomers', who have no previous experience of the local context. These are likely to be new expressions of church that have moved into the area and have yet to make significant connections with the local community habitat. Expressions of church and missional communities may be 'Citizens', those who have established networks and connections. These are likely to be time-honoured churches and Christian communities who have been present for a number of years.

Dwelling patterns

Dwelling patterns have to do with how present expressions of church or missional communities are. They may be 'Resident', living within the geographical context. Such Christian communities will have frequent opportunities to engage with the residential, business, educational and civic communities in the spaces and places of their local community habitat. For example, a church that is resident may have a high proportion of its congregation living or working locally, or it may have a strong presence in the local community owing to local groups using its buildings or because it has a programme of events and services. Expressions of church and missional communities may be 'Commuters', engaging with their local habitat less frequently, dipping in and out in different ways. A church that opens its doors only on Sundays may well have less of a presence, and a church to which most of the congregation travel in from other communities for worship and events will have more of a Commuter personality.

As outlined in the *Anvil* article, there are four combinations of dwelling pattern that describe the process of contextual inhabitation: Citizen Resident, Citizen Commuter, Incomer Resident, and Incomer Commuter. Citizen Residents will be very well known and very present and will be achieving contextual inhabitation. Incomer Commuters who are not very known or present will find it much harder to achieve this. It's important to note that these definitions may not be static. As a new missional community establishes itself, it will become more known and more present. A church that for whatever reason pulls up its drawbridge and focuses primarily on its own congregation may become less known and less present.

In mapping the inhabitation of a mixed ecology, it is useful to find out how known and present the individual expressions of church and missional communities are and then to look at how this describes the system as a whole. First of all, doing this will help Christian communities to understand more of one another's identities and practices as they seek to grow in connectivity. For example, if a Citizen Resident church (very known and very present) is wanting to increase connectivity with an Incomer Resident church (not as known yet very present), it will be helpful to be aware of their commonality and difference, perhaps through drawing on the 'gathering' and 'connecting' stages of the mixed ecology journey. As one is known and one is less known, it may be that the Citizen aspect of one can inform the Incomer aspect of the other by making introductions and helping the Incomer to get to know the local community habitat. Likewise, the Incomer can also help the Citizen to see things in a different way by offering a fresh perspective, which can be valuable in shifting assumptions or in recognising aspects of change in the local community if they have been in a place for a long time. Yet, in this scenario, both expressions of church are Residents, meaning that there will be more opportunity to work together. This paves the way for the possibility of collaboration and co-creating as they adopt the principles of recognising, resourcing and resilience.

Second, mapping the contextual inhabitation of a whole ecosystem can reveal the overall dynamics of the collective expressions of church and missional communities. If an ecosystem has a high number of Incomer Commuters, it is likely to be harder and take more time to develop connectivity, as there is less opportunity to be in proximity to one another. If there are high numbers of very established Citizen Residents with only a few Incomer Commuters, relational dynamics could make it harder for the Incomers to be accepted into the ecosystem, as a mentality of 'We've always done it this way' could be present. Conversely, if the ecosystem has a high number of Incomers and few Citizens, the Christian communities who have been present for a long time may feel overwhelmed. It may therefore take them longer to build connectivity.

Whatever the combination of starting points and dwelling patterns, being aware of the dynamics of how known and present the components of the mixed ecology are will be very helpful in breaking down resistance and perceiving opportunities for connectivity.

The posture of inhabitation

As expressions of church and missional communities seek to inhabit their ecclesial and missional spaces and places, three postures of inhabitation come to the fore: abiding, innovating and enabling. When different expressions of church cultivate these attitudes and ways of being, greater integration and a higher likelihood of connectivity are made possible.

Abiding

The son of a friend of mine has just started secondary school and is studying 'Immersive Mandarin'. This means that, as well as a language class, three other subjects are also taught in Mandarin, such as maths or physical education. The students are exposed to a number of different approaches and learning styles, which is apparently really effective and is bringing great results. Often the best way to learn a language is to immerse yourself fully by abiding in the culture and practices of the place where it is used.

The notion of abiding means to remain or to endure. The New King James Version of the Bible uses this language in the famous passage about the vine and the branches, where Jesus charges his disciples to 'abide in Me, and I in you. As the branch cannot bear fruit of itself, unless it abides in the vine, neither can you, unless you abide in Me' (John 15:4, NKJV).

This language of 'abiding', then, is about living, dwelling and being rooted in Jesus, who is the sturdy branch of the grapevine. If we remain or abide in Jesus we will bear much fruit, for apart from him we can do nothing. More than this, the branches that are deemed dead will be cut off and thrown into the fire. In spiritual terms, abiding is to be fully immersed in God and for him to be fully immersed in us. If we are to inhabit ecclesiological and missiological habitats, we will also need to abide in them.

First, this involves a commitment to radical participation as a community of believers. I have to confess that one of my pet peeves is when church leaders say to the resident congregation, 'Thank you for joining us today'. I'm sure I have said this myself as a church leader in the past, but I heard it again recently and it really made me feel uncomfortable. I think this is because, if you analyse it, it doesn't really reflect a community of people who are collectively inhabiting their space and place of worship. Who is being thanked, exactly? As it's being said by the person at the front of the church, it must be the congregation. If this is the case, then 'us' must be the people at the front of church, the leaders. And if we are being thanked for joining them, does it imply that they are in charge and we are merely being invited to join in? Although this may be true of some churches, it's not the kind of church that I want to be part of, or that I think is needed. As Lings would argue, a church that is seeking to inhabit the seven sacred spaces is a more collaborative and integrated community where all are abiding and rooted in their ecclesial habitat.

Of course, we need leaders to lead, but their role should rather be that of enabling others (we will come to this later). It's a culture of 'being with', not 'doing for' or 'doing to'.

This brings us to the theme of being and doing, which we touched on earlier. During the Covid-19 pandemic when all physical meetings had to stop, I hosted a weekly drop-in on Zoom for pioneering church leaders. After we had met a couple of times, it became clear that much of the ministry of those on the call revolved around 'doing': physical gathering, shared community practices, social entrepreneurial activity. When this admittedly good stuff was prevented by lockdown, it revealed that the abiding roots of some were very shallow. The posture of 'being' – of journeying with others, pastoral care, careful listening and praying for the needs of those around you – wasn't always as evident. In other publications I have explored the idea that perhaps, in such an activist world, 'being should be the new doing'. By this I mean that, rather than placing high value on outward activity, we should place high value on missional, pastoral and discipling relationships, which in themselves may become our doing, or in monastic terms our 'work' or garden. For the church to grow and flourish, it needs deep roots: prayerful and godly leaders and confident 'Jesus-shaped' disciples who are missionally literate, a people of God who can live out the missio Dei. To do this, they will need well-established spiritual foundations. This is what I think is at the heart of what Jesus is talking about with the vine and the branches: abide in me as I abide in you and you will bear much fruit.

Graham Tomlin, however, sounds a helpful cautionary note.

> I'm not sure I'd want to push a contrast between 'being' and 'doing' too far. Doing always emerges from being, and being is shaped by doing, just as action always emerges from our prayer, stillness and worship of the God of Jesus Christ. The quality of our presence to God and to others is crucial in all that we do, but an emphasis purely on being can lead to a passivity and presumption that does not help us. Jesus was always 'about his Father's business' and so should we be.[8]

I have recently been reading about schema therapy, which draws on a range of different aspects of neurophysiology in its approach. At its heart is the premise that we all establish life traps or life commandments in childhood, given to us consciously or unconsciously by our primary caregivers. Examples of these might be 'I will always get it wrong', 'I am not good enough', 'I will be rejected by others', or 'I will never achieve what I need to'. These give rise to schema narratives. If we carry these with us into adulthood, they will influence our behaviour, thoughts and decision making. One of the ways to counter life commandments is to identify the schemas that have been formed. Dr Jeffrey Young has identified eighteen schemas.[9] If one of your life commandments is 'I will always make mistakes', the schemas attached to it might be unrelenting standards (needing everything to be perfect) or defectiveness (feeling that there is something wrong with you). If your life commandment is 'I will never achieve what I need to', the schemas attached to it might be failure (I will never get things right) or subjugation (people pleasing). Progress is made by identifying the life commandments and schemas that are at play and replacing them with new life commandments such as 'I am good enough' or 'I am loved'.

Without stretching the analogy too far, I wonder if local church communities can have life commandments and schemas that may have an impact on their opinions and behaviour. The distinctive nature and personalities of different expressions of church may be formed by their collective experiences of church. If we are to build greater connectivity within an integrated mixed ecology, it will be essential to address any schematic frameworks that exist, as they will skew the way Christian communities view themselves and therefore view others. For example, a church might have a life commandment of 'Certain other traditions of church are bad', born from schemas such as mistrust (the belief that others are abusive, manipulative, selfish or looking to hurt or use you, and thus are not to be trusted) or entitlement (the belief that you are special and that you do not have to follow the rules like other people; an exaggerated focus on superiority for the purposes of having power or control). These schema frameworks may be formed from a community's negative experiences or by those of its leaders who influence it in some way.

As already noted, growing an integrated mixed ecology can be hard to do in reality, as prejudice, misconceptions and misinformation can hamper connectivity. Building a mixed ecology will be greatly aided if the expressions of church and missional communities dig deep into their ecclesiological and missiological psyches to see what schemas are present that could negatively affect their opinions of and behaviour towards others in the ecosystem. This is where the posture of abiding comes in: it will enable this work to happen as each Christian community seeks to inhabit their spaces and places more profoundly. As expressions of church remain in Jesus, who is the vine that enables their branches to bear good fruit, they will also benefit, however painfully, from allowing any branches that aren't bearing good fruit to be pruned. The work of the Holy Spirit in revealing and rewriting any ecclesiological or missiological schemas will be vital in this work of abiding.

Innovating

The posture of innovating is also important for inhabiting a mixed ecology of church. I think innovation provokes a bit of a mixed reaction within the church today. Some see it as essential in our post-modern, post-pandemic times, while others may be suspicious of reinventing the wheel or innovating for the sake of innovating. Some will enjoy working from a blank canvas while others will be better working to a brief or developing something that already exists. For the mixed ecology to grow, innovation will be needed as new connections, relationships and partnerships begin to form. Connectivity in itself has innovation as part of its DNA, as new ways of working together are found.

A friend of mine is an artist and a neurologist and talks about the process of creativity simply being the joining of one dot to another, seeing what exists and bringing them together to create something new. In her view, people who are neurodivergent can be especially good at innovation and creativity as they not only join the dots in a different way but can also see more dots. In the context of the mixed ecology, dots might be people, places, churches, ideas or resources. There is a call to raise up the creative thinkers and to amplify the voices of the neurodivergent, who will be able to see new ways of connecting that others might not be able to see. But everyone, no matter who they are, can be involved in this.

Talking point

To see what my conversion partners thought about inhabiting innovation, I asked them, 'In what ways is the mixed ecology of church a fruitful place for inhabiting innovation?'

Terri: Most of my passion and drive for innovation and ministry have stemmed from existing challenges in areas that mattered to me, that is, current church forms not connecting the gospel with young people. Exploring the challenge that surfaces, gaining a deeper understanding of what it is and why it matters and experimenting with how to address it can feed back into existing spaces in a fruitful way. When space to explore and experiment can be created alongside inherited structures (with permission to go off the map), all parties win. This means that the unstructured way has support, the existing structure learns about what is emerging, and (if they can truly hear each other) a new vision for the future might be imagined. It is also important to note that this is really hard to do.

Ian: I welcome the concept of the mixed ecology as giving greater respect and confidence and a sense of unity to both traditional and experimental forms of church, and to the many varied emphases present within those loose categories. Rewilding, refounding and reimaging will all require an innovative approach that is both bold and humble, rooted in love for God and for neighbour.

Graham: The parish system has always been a moving, living, breathing organism rather than a fixed bureaucratic structure. Over the centuries it has shifted boundaries and developed new worshipping communities, such as chantry chapels, chapels of ease, wayside shrines, and more recently Bishops' Mission Orders. I remain convinced that if the parish system did not exist, we would want to invent it, because the idea of a church community in every town, village and suburb across the country is unique and irreplaceable. However, it needs to develop and evolve as it has always done, so, to me, the mixed ecology really is nothing new. It is simply a way of describing the continuing evolution of the parish system into the future.[10]

Change is never easy. People tend to embrace it by adopting new forms of behaviour and practices over time. We can't effect massive change all at once, and if we do, things tend to get bumpy. There is value in starting with small changes and making it easy for people to do hard things.[11]

So the mixed ecology can grow through the posture of innovation. More specifically, growth can happen by virtue of the very collective nature of the mixed ecology, as innovations are fostered that might not have arisen in isolation. For example, my first pioneering role was in a united benefice of two churches in Central London, comprising a theatre church and a church with a choral Book of Common Prayer (BCP) tradition. Both were wonderful in their own way but they were very different, and, looking back, I think they did help each other to innovate. The creativity of the theatre church came out in the development of a very popular all-age worship service at the BCP church. The beautiful music of the BCP church provided wonderful classical concerts at the theatre church. The posture of innovation within a mixed ecology can be a catalyst for new things to grow, with the old and the new working together. I call this the aspiration spiral, which can be described as follows.

The aspiration spiral

In developing a new idea or project, there are often four stages or attitudes in its development that move it from start-up to maturity. This is a journey from aspiration to possibility, to capability, and finally into wisdom. We see these attitudes in the character and nature of God:

Now to Him who is able to [carry out His purpose and] do superabundantly more than all that we dare ask or think [infinitely beyond our greatest prayers, hopes, or dreams], according to His power that is at work within us, to Him be the glory in the church and in Christ Jesus throughout all generations forever and ever. Amen. (Ephesians 3:20–1, AMP)

Aspiration: a creator God who 'can carry out his purposes', which we see poured into creation though his creativity. God's DNA permeates the created world. I often look at the natural world and am amazed by its order, precision and intricacy. This also includes God's aspiration for salvation ('to him be glory in the church and in Christ Jesus'), his desire to redeem humanity through sending the sacrificial gift of his own Son.

Possibility: an eternal God who can 'do superabundantly more than all that we dare ask', who makes the impossible possible. God is outside time: he is the alpha and the omega, who was and is and is to come. There is always more to discover as we journey with God, and there is always more that God wants to do in us and through us.

Capability: an omnipotent God who can do all things 'according to His power that is at work within us'. We worship a God who has the power to create, to do the miraculous, to conquer death itself. Many of my family and friends can tell amazing stories about the wonderful things God has done in their lives, ranging from healings to supernatural encounters and divine guidance. God is also an omnipresent God who is in all things, according to 'His power that is at work within us'.

Wisdom: an omniscient God, who can do 'more than all that we dare ask or think [infinitely beyond our greatest prayers, hopes, or dreams]'. God's ways are not our ways and his thoughts are higher than our thoughts. There are so many moments in life when God's timing and provision are just right, and so different from the ways in which we try to work it out for ourselves.

The aspiration spiral takes these four themes and provides this framework for us to move from start-up to maturity.

From: Start-up

1 *Aspiration*: where a new idea occurs, a question is posed, and a desire to start up or to bring something into being is identified.
2 *Possibility*: where there is openness to what could be, exploration, trial and error, research and development.
3 *Capability*: where there is increased ability, clarity and process, where the idea has taken shape, and the question is being answered.
4 *Wisdom*: where lessons have been learned, there is deeper understanding, and the idea or the question has matured.

To: Maturity

This aspirational journey often benefits from projects and communities that are already in a mature phase of development. Such projects can also often benefit from projects in a start-up phase. To gain this insight in both directions, it can be helpful to hold a 'chaordic' space between projects or expressions of church that are at different stages of growth and development. The concept of 'chaordic' was developed by the Art of Hosting movement.[12] It combines chaos and order, allowing for creative 'chaos', which brings the new, and boundaried 'order', which brings clarity and direction. Their joint forces can powerfully enable a task or project to move forward. A chaordic space can help each of the four stages of development (aspiration, possibility, capability and wisdom) to inform one another for their mutual benefit (see Table 1).

Table 1

	Aspiration	*Possibility*	*Capability*	*Wisdom*
Benefit to start-up project from mature project	Help in shaping the idea	Help in discovering what has and hasn't been possible	Help in knowing what has and hasn't worked before	Help in honing collective wisdom
Benefit to mature project from start-up project	Inspiration to develop further	Inspiration to expand ability and know how	Inspiration to see what more could be possible	Inspiration to have a new idea

This can become a continuous cycle of development (as shown in Figure 10). A **start-up** project joins the spiral and receives inspiration from more mature projects. As it reaches maturity itself, it can continue its journey by moving from wisdom back towards aspiration again. When it reaches aspiration, it starts this cycle all over again and the spiral keeps going. It may be that the project reinvents itself or that there are aspects of the project that are innovated and adapted to keep it relevant and/or to continue in its development. Likewise, a **mature project** can join the cycle by moving from wisdom back towards aspiration again and in doing so it can find inspiration to develop itself further, beginning to see what else could be possible as it changes and adapts. In this sense the spiral continues. The projects that learn from one another could be the same two projects over a long period of time, or they could be different projects at different times, as long as the stages of development align in an appropriate way. Generally, the start-up project will initiate this process by seeking to work with a mature project – unless the mature project recognises it has reached a place of stagnation or plateau, and so seeks out a start-up.

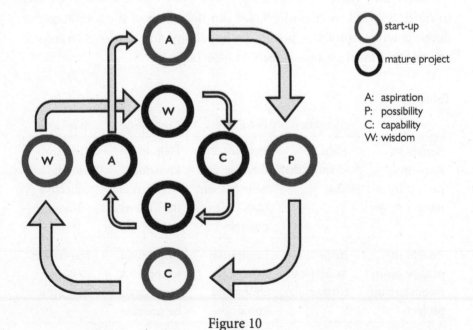

start-up

mature project

A: aspiration
P: possibility
C: capability
W: wisdom

Figure 10

This process is very helpful in fostering innovation within the mixed ecology of church. New emerging expressions of church and missional initiatives can bring a fresh perspective while mature expressions of church and missional communities can bring important local knowledge and an established rhythm and pattern of worship, tradition and mission. Think of an established time-honoured expression of church and a café church in the same parish or neighbourhood. Members of the time-honoured church see a need to extend the reach of the parish and want to start a new Christian community in parallel with the existing church. The aspiration of the café church may seek the wisdom of the time-honoured church by exploring how to develop habits of prayer and discipleship. The time-honoured church may have much to offer in this area as a result of many years of supporting the spirituality of the worshipping community. Likewise, the time-honoured church may have an aspiration with which it seeks help from the café church. For example, if new housing has been built in the area, it might want to learn how to continue to engage with the local community as it changes. Being embedded in that local community, the café church may have wisdom in this area, bringing a different perspective that could benefit the missional vision of the time-honoured church. As both move through the spiral, the hope is that the mature expression of church sees new possibilities and forms new aspirations and the new Christian community grows in capability and wisdom. The spiral continues, and as it does so the posture of innovation is embedded by the relationships of the mixed ecology. If this happens with multiple churches in the ecosystem, there could be rich learning opportunities for all.

Enabling

The ability to enable the leadership of others is an increasingly vital quality in ministry. The Church of England has many aims that are served by its existing leaders identifying, encouraging and supporting the development of new and emerging (mostly lay) leaders. For example, there is the goal of growing 10,000 new worshipping communities by 2030, many of which will be lay-led, and the 'Setting God's People Free' and 'Everyday Faith' initiatives seek to encourage the growth of lay ministry. In order to have the confidence to flourish, new leaders will need the encouragement of existing ones.

If you look at the qualities identified by the Church of England as important for the discernment and formation of lay and ordained ministers, you will see that many make reference to enabling others. Reflecting further on the importance of this, I developed something I call 'the enabling leadership cycle', which seeks to offer encouragement through a framework by which leaders can better enable the ministry of others.

The Cycle

Figure 11 outlines the enabling leadership cycle and has two interconnecting elements: the enabling leader and the emerging leader(s).

The enabling leader is someone who has oversight of others or is the catalyst for the development of others, and so has an opportunity to cultivate new leaders and to nurture existing ones. To do this effectively, the enabling leader will need to grow in their openness to others, which will also help them to expand their awareness of themselves in relation to others. This will improve their enabling attitude and therefore their desire and ability to allow others to take the lead.

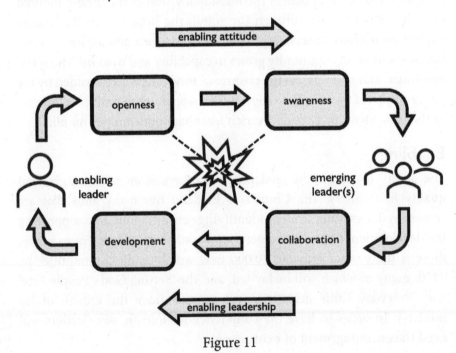

Figure 11

Emerging leader(s) are people who are in the orbit of the enabling leader. With an attitude of openness and awareness, the enabling leader seeks to provide space for collaboration with those in their community who are potential or emerging leaders. This brings opportunity for leadership development. The emerging leaders will mature in their leadership as their desire and ability to lead increase.

These processes don't happen in isolation. The space in the middle of the cycle allows for an interplay between the growth of enabling and emerging leaders. For example, as the enabling leader develops an attitude of openness to others, an opportunity for collaboration with the emerging leaders is created. As the enabling leader develops an attitude of self-awareness, an opportunity for the leadership development of emerging leaders is created. And the cycle goes on: as the enabling leader's attitude changes, they will be more directly engaged in collaboration and leadership development. As the emerging leaders grow in their leadership, they will develop their attitude of openness and awareness as they begin to take the lead. This is very useful when applied to an integrated mixed ecology of church. Individual church or mission leaders may well enable other leaders, but the process also works collectively, as church communities seek to enable other communities. More than this, when local community habitats are inhabited well by local worshipping communities, there will be a need for churches to enable local communities and, perhaps more radically, for local communities to enable leadership in the churches.

I was talking recently to someone who was trying to persuade the church leader they work for to commission a power audit. This, I imagine, is a process of exploring where power lies, who holds it, and how freely it flows within the organisation. In the institutional church, where power lies at the top and cascades down the layers, we have tended to create tall structures of power. This sets up an 'us and them' culture that can make ministry relationships fairly transactional. We see this in the national and the local church. I remember a clergy friend of mine moaning that their congregation never volunteered to do anything or took any initiative, meaning that the clergy and leadership team ended up having to do everything. I don't know that congregation: it might be that they just didn't want to help, were too busy or didn't have the know-how, but whatever the case I wondered whether the specific power structures in place (set up or perpetuated by the leaders) were not enabling the members of the church to be more proactive and involved. If the leaders do all the groundwork and just invite people to join in, people can feel quite disempowered. It is better to foster a culture of engaging and enabling, which will involve the people at the top letting go of power and growing a model of leadership based on a flat hierarchy.

If different expressions of Christian community are going to recognise, resource and give resilience to one another in the integrated mixed ecology of church, it is crucial that they hold to a posture of enabling. The ecosystem will need to look at where power is held and how they are seeking to enable one another as a community of churches. In his book *Multicultural Kingdom*, Harvey Kwiyani likens the church to a smorgasbord with lots of different things making up each individual church.[13] This is in the context of his discourse on growing multicultural church communities, but the analogy is helpful in thinking about the mixed ecology too. Instead of a smorgasbord, he argues that we often tend to see church as a smoothie, where people need to conform. He argues in favour of diversity, expressed as 'mission is no longer from here to there, but from everywhere to everywhere'.

We can take this further. Sharon Prentis, Deputy Director of the Church of England's Racial Justice Unit, speaks powerfully about the difference between multicultural and intercultural. The first implies diversity but the second implies integrated diversity. Intercultural can be defined as living together with interdependence where there is a community-wide and intentional commitment to building a new social, cultural and religious reality out of several cultures. This entails a cross-cultural commitment on the part of each to learning from one another and opening themselves to the possibility that God works through difference.[14]

Again, Sharon Prentis's comments are made in the context of the intercultural church, but can translate to the work of connectivity within the mixed ecology. To move from 'multi-church' to 'inter-church', we need to address the presence of entitlement and power, which are often part of our church culture. In replacing these, we need an emphasis on the values of humility, sacrifice, grace and so forth.[15] The key question in developing a posture of enabling others in the mixed ecology is, 'What power do we have to lay down in order for "inter" to happen?' In intercultural terms, diversity without relationship and commitment becomes no more than tokenism. The same can be said about the integrated mixed ecology: a tokenistic partnering and connectivity isn't going to get us very far and will probably end up pushing expressions of church further apart rather than drawing them closer together.

A posture of enabling should also be focused on those who are a minority in a space, the powerless and voiceless, those who lack confidence. Often this starts with creating a culture of welcome. Having visited a number of new churches recently, as a church leader in the pews I've really noticed what makes a good welcome. If there is too little, you feel as if you shouldn't be there or even that people don't want you to be there. Yet when there is too much, it can feel overwhelming, especially if you might be new to churchy things or just trying to work out where you fit in. I have been in a few churches where the welcomer or church leader at the door has pulled out a notebook to write my details down so they won't forget them. I understand why they might do this, but it makes me feel uncomfortable. Who else is listed in the notebook? Where is this notebook kept? What will happen to my information? I'm sure it's meant well, but it's also disempowering, and the information balance is uneven: do I know as much detail about the person welcoming me as they now know about me? There is a subtle but very big difference between saying, 'Hello, what's your name?' and, 'Hello, my name is x; what's your name?' The first suggests superiority while the second promotes shared information and equality of power.[16] Those who are a minority in a space and place will value being made to feel welcome in this way.

If we can inhabit welcome well, we will be able to empower one another within the integrated mixed ecology. For example, imagine that different expressions of church and missional communities are engaging with the stages of the mixed ecology journey outlined in chapter 2 and are looking to put up 'tents' and meeting places. This is not going to go well if the bigger, more monied or powerful Christian communities launch in with an 'And who are *you*?' approach to the smaller, newer or more fragile communities. Instead, an empowering and equalising attitude of welcome will be a foundation for collaboration and for the enabling of one another. It is also important for allowing innovation to flow from the edges, from people not in leadership roles or situations of power. It allows the ecosystem to be supported and nurtured as new leaders are developed, as well as being a catalyst for the partnering of aspiration and wisdom.

By recognising the ecclesial and local community habitats that make up a local mixed ecology, by looking at the ways in which they are inhabited and by cultivating the postures of abiding, innovating and enabling, we can begin to develop connectivity and form an integrated mixed ecology.

Questions

1 Which of the seven sacred spaces are most at play in the expression of church or missional community that you inhabit?
2 How aware are you of the starting points and dwelling patterns of the different organisms within your local mixed ecology? How could the posture of abiding enable deeper roots to be grown?
3 How can a culture of enabling leadership be built within the different organisms of the local mixed ecology?
4 How is power inhabited within the worshipping communities in your local area? How might it move from being 'multi' to 'inter'?

Contributors

Ian Adams is Chaplain at Ridley Hall, Cambridge and Spirituality Lead at Church Mission Society.

Graham Tomlin is the Director of the Centre for Cultural Witness, based in Lambeth Palace. He was Bishop of Kensington from 2015 to 2022 and is President of St Mellitus College.

Terri Elton is Dean of Academic Affairs and Professor of Leadership at Luther Seminary, Minnesota, USA.

4

Leading a mixed ecology

The more I have worked with churches and more recently in the area of theological education, the more I am convinced that the transformation of the church will come about through its leaders. This is not to say that they have to do all the work. Far from it: the bulk of the ministry will be done by those in the pews, padded chairs or wherever they find themselves sitting. But if the leadership doesn't establish the right culture and climate for a vibrant, healthy church, it just won't happen. Leadership, of course, comes in all shapes and sizes, which makes sense as our expressions of church and missional communities all look different from one another too. To think about what kind of leadership might be needed to develop an integrated mixed ecology, we will look at four areas of leadership: the mixed ecology charism, what a mixed ecology minister looks like, how to launch and land, and the importance of collaboration.

The mixed ecology charism

Leadership in the mixed ecology can take a number of forms. The mixed ecology charism uses a framework of four traits to help to discern the calling and practice of a leader within the mixed ecology. First comes the question 'Why?'. This asks the leader what their ministry vocation and passion is, whom they feel called to reach and minister to, and why. It speaks of what drives them, catches their attention, gets them out of bed in the mornings. Second comes the question 'What?'. This asks the leader what they feel called to lead, start or oversee. It is explored by using the language of legacy and founding, and speaks of the work they are interested in and able to lead. Third comes the question 'How?'. This asks the leader what their approach and methodology are. It is explored by using the language of attractional and contextual, and speaks of the way in which they lead and minister. Fourth comes the question 'Where?'. This asks the leader how 'present' and 'known' they need to be to fulfil what God is calling them to do. It is explored using the concept of contextual inhabitation, which we looked at in chapter 3, and speaks of the starting points and dwelling patterns into which the leader is called.

Practitioners and overseers

Table 2 is a summary of the different ways these four traits can be expressed.

Table 2

Why?	What?
Legacy Starter	Time-honoured
Founding Starter	Seed
Developer	Runner
Community Entrepreneur	Plant
Advocate	Bridge-back
	Enterprise

How?	Where?
Innovator	Citizen Resident
Adapter	Citizen Commuter
Replicator	Incomer Resident
Curator	Incomer Commuter

Some will be called to be mixed ecology practitioners, holding different expressions of church together at the same time; others will have a calling to a specific part of the ecology. Some will be called to be overseers of and advocates for those working in a similar or different part of the ecology. Some may inhabit a mixture of being a practitioner and an overseer in one or several spheres of the ecology. For example, an incumbent of a traditional church may oversee others leading a new Christian community, or someone leading a new Christian community may oversee leaders in other new Christian communities.

The four traits of the mixed ecology charism are considered below in more detail. It's important to note that some leaders may inhabit several of the categories within a given trait. This is right and proper, as leadership can be multilayered and also change over time. In my experience, however, most people will identify with a primary category in each trait.

Why?

Founding Starters: are good at starting new distinct things in new places well away from the reach of the established church.

Legacy Starters: are good at starting new distinct things in parallel with an existing church and within its setting, seeking to extend the missional reach.

Developers: are gifted at nurturing and serving an existing worshipping community. There is less emphasis on starting from scratch, and they will often build on the legacy of others. This could be in a new expression of church or an established or time-honoured church.

Community Entrepreneurs: are good at engaging in social transformation and are mission-focused and entrepreneurial. They are first on the scene and, although they are not necessarily called to start a new worshipping community, their primary gift is to innovate and to share their faith.

Advocates: are good at enabling others in their ministry, publicly supporting and championing them and their work.

What?

Time-honoured: a Christian community that has existed for a long time with a local theology that each generation builds on.

Seed: a Christian community that will be grown some distance away from the existing church, with minimal connections, drawing on a contextual 'serving-first' approach.[1]

Runner: a Christian community that will be grown within the setting of the existing church with strong supportive links, drawing on a contextual 'serving-first' approach.[2]

Plant: a Christian community that will be grown some distance away from the sending church, with supportive connections, drawing on an attractional, worshipping 'serving-first' approach.

Bridge-back: a new missional community that provides a pathway (intentionally or unintentionally) back into an existing expression of church.[3]

Enterprise: a missional activity that forms community and may lay ecclesial foundations, but doesn't necessarily form into a church itself.

How?

The language of innovator, adapter and replicator is taken from the Pioneer Spectrum.[4] The term 'curator' can usefully be added, as they have a particular role to play as well.

Innovator: will start from a blank canvas, engaging in original thinking as they draw from the context around them.

Adapter: will be responsive to the context by borrowing from other things they have seen and making them their own.

Replicator: will start new things where a successful model of church can be repeated, often created in the culture of those leading it.

Curator: will oversee and hold the vision together, drawing in what is needed for growth.

Where?

Here is a summary of what was explored in detail in chapter 3.

Citizen Resident: will be very known and very present. They will have lived in their community for some time and have established connections in the missional context.

Citizen Commuter: will be very known and somewhat present. They will have established connections within the missional context, but will minister in a different context from the one in which they live, and often travel between these two communities.

Incomer Resident: will be somewhat known and very present. They will be new to the context, without established missional connections, and will minister within the community where they are living.

Incomer Commuter: will be somewhat known and somewhat present. They will live in one context and minister in a neighbouring community in which they are not yet known and are without established missional connections.

Who?

By working through these traits, combining the why, what, how and where, we can discover more about 'who' we are called to be as leaders and 'where' our ministry lies within the ecosystem of the mixed ecology (see Figure 12). This can reveal more about 'how' to live out our calling. It is also useful to look at what other types of ministry are close by in the ecosystem – this can show who might be important to work alongside or indicate ways to expand our own calling or ministry. It also gives a sense of how our calling is part of the bigger picture and supports the work of God in wider terms. It is important to note that the ministries shown here are by no means an exhaustive list; many more could be placed within this leadership ecosystem.

Examples

Here are a few worked examples, which can show the value of the mixed ecology charism.

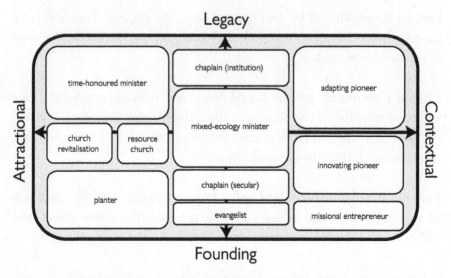

Figure 12

Parish priest (time-honoured ministry)

Why?
Primary trait: Developer
Secondary traits: Advocate/Community Entrepreneur

What?
Primary trait: Time-honoured
Secondary traits: Enterprise

How?
Primary trait: Curator
Secondary traits: Adapter

Where?
Primary trait: Citizen Resident
Secondary traits: Citizen Commuter

The goal of this leader is to develop what already exists. They also have a desire to be an advocate for others who are working in the local ecosystem, perhaps raising up local planters and pioneers to start runners and small planting projects. They have a passion for community entrepreneurialism, wanting to think creatively about mission. They are probably leading a time-honoured church and also developing missional projects, perhaps a food bank or a social enterprise. Their primary way of working is as a curator overseeing and releasing the ministry of others. As an adapter, they are involved in observing and borrowing from other projects they have seen and shaping them to fit their own ministry context. Lastly, as a Citizen Resident they are present and known in their local community, living and ministering with the people they are leading and seeking to reach. Their work in social enterprise may take them into new spaces within the local community, meaning that they are not always present in that space so will occupy the trait of a Commuter.

Lay pioneer (adapting pioneer)

Why?
Primary trait: Legacy Starter
Secondary traits: Developer

What?
Primary trait: Runner
Secondary traits: Bridge-back

How?
Primary trait: Adapter
Secondary traits: Innovator

Where?
Primary trait: Citizen Resident
Secondary traits: Citizen Commuter

The motivation of this leader is to develop something new to extend the reach of the local church in the community and connect with people who won't step over the threshold of the time-honoured church. They also have a desire to be a developer because, as well as starting new things, they will want to expand and mature them over time. They are likely to be leading a fresh expression of church such as a café church, Messy

Church or a new Christian community meeting in a local situation. It's likely that they will also be attending the time-honoured church that supports them, and so could also be building an aspect of a new worshipping community that bridges people back to the time-honoured church. The traits of runner and bridge-back can co-exist in the same fresh expression. Some new people who find their way in may stay, while for others the new community might be a stepping stone into the time-honoured church. This leader's primary way of working is as an adapter, again involved in observing and borrowing from other projects they have seen and shaping them for their own ministry context. Their secondary trait indicates they may be working as an emerging innovator. As they adapt and gain confidence, stepping out into new things, their ability to 'think outside the box' may grow and original thought may increase. Last, as a Citizen Resident they are present and known in their local community, living and ministering with the people they are leading and seeking to reach. The new people who attend the runner are likely to be the neighbours and acquaintances of the lay pioneer. As they are also attending the time-honoured church, there is a sense of commuting in and out of the new worshipping community.

Contextual chaplain (secular chaplain)
Why?
Primary trait: Founding Starter
Secondary traits: Community Entrepreneur

What?
Primary trait: Seed
Secondary traits: Enterprise

How?
Primary trait: Innovator
Secondary traits: Curator

Where?
Primary trait: Citizen Commuter
Secondary traits: Incomer Commuter

The longing of this leader is to develop something new and deep within the secular missionary context. They also have a desire to be a curator, by overseeing the work and ministry of others in this missional space. They are likely to be leading a chaplaincy within a community of people with a common interest or need (beach surfers, the homeless community, a new housing estate). Their second trait of enterprise reveals that they have started something new, perhaps responding to a practical need (e.g. health or substance abuse problems in those living on the streets). This could be a charity or a self-supporting chaplaincy. Again, the trait of seed shows their ability and desire to start something new, probably out of a season of listening to, loving and serving the people around them. As they are chaplains, there will be a strong focus on social and pastoral care, with a deep interest in the lives of the people with whom they are forming relationships. Their primary way of working is as an innovator, which again maps on to being a starter and Community Entrepreneur, growing a seed or an enterprise of some kind. The trait of working as a curator may be present in gathering local agency partners or social action charities, with or alongside whom they minister. Last, as a Citizen Commuter they are well known and somewhat present. They may be very well known in the local community but not live directly in that community. As an innovator, they may in time reach out to a new people group as well, and if so would be an Incomer Commuter, but as they get to know people they have the potential to become a Citizen Commuter.

A mixed ecology of leadership

We have seen that the dynamics of the mixed ecology are not just about the spaces and places that are inhabited. They are also about the leaders and ministers within them. Over the past seven or eight years, I have been teaching in theological colleges and running local diocesan training on the mixed ecology. One really fascinating exercise I have led involves mapping out the leadership mixed-ecology ecosystem on the floor and, through a series of questions, asking people to stand in the appropriate space and then explore the mixed ecology from a particular leadership perspective. I've done this with groups of varying sizes, from ten students to 200 clergy at a diocesan conference, often with similar results.

First, I ask people to stand in the space that best describes their ministry, their passion and their 'who?'. Depending on the group's make-up, the majority of people tend to stand in the time-honoured ministry space, which is legacy and attractional or 'Country Garden' (see chapter 2). This is mostly because that describes the majority of churches in the Church of England. Some will stand in a pioneering and planting space. Some will stand in the middle, which can describe a mixed ecology minister (we will come to that later in this chapter). I then ask people to look around and observe where others are standing in the ecosystem. It's a powerful moment when people acknowledge that there are those who are in a similar leadership space and those who are clearly in a different one from themselves. It affirms that difference is OK and is in fact an important aspect of the mixed ecology. I then ask people to talk to the people around them and note their commonality. I ask people to find someone who is in a different part of the ecosystem and talk to them to find out why they are standing there and what similarities and differences exist between them. Generally, there is always something they have in common, such a calling to serve their local community, to pray, to reach out in mission. It often happens that the differences in their leadership traits (the why, what, how and where) are revealed. This is a wonderful learning opportunity to build recognition across the mixed ecology.

Second, with people back in their original positions, I ask them to stand in the space within the mixed ecology that best describes the expressions of church and missional projects that they lead. At this point some stay where they are and some move. The people who move often go to a related part of the ecosystem. If they were standing in time-honoured ministry (legacy, attractional), they might move to resource church planting or to parish pioneering. Some, however, move to a totally different part of the ecosystem. This often prompts a meaningful discussion about how they can best use their charism if it isn't directly matching the place where they are in leadership.

Third, I ask people to indicate whether they think the church or project they are leading needs to grow into a different part of the ecosystem to allow it to develop. Here, many people will move to another part of the ecosystem, indicating that they think the church needs to learn from other ways of doing things in order to flourish. I call this 'launching and landing' (we will explore this later in the chapter). This shows again the need for an integrated and connected mixed ecology, demonstrating that expressions of church are not static and that they do need the resourcing and resilience that the mixed ecology can offer. It is, therefore, important to look at what other types of ministry exist close by in the local mixed ecology. As I said earlier, this could either indicate who might be important to work alongside or pinpoint ways in which you can expand your own calling, ministry or church community. For example, church revitalisation, resource church, mixed ecology ministry, chaplaincy (institutional, e.g. school) and distinctive deacon are all close to one another in the leadership ecosystem. How could one or some of these be a possible support or a future area of ministry focus?

Another aspect of mixed ecology leadership is that combinations sometimes form that draw on two different leadership approaches. Over the past twenty years or so, the contextual pioneers and attractional church planters have been fairly siloed, both holding to their own preferred way of doing things. Yet over the past few years this has changed, with more planned work to bring these different leadership communities together to learn from one another through local partnerships, conferences and shared training. However, I also think that a new approach to growing new Christian communities is emerging, combining both leadership approaches. Attractional planters tend to become more contextual the more they plant, and contextual pioneers are looking more at the sustainability and long-term ecclesiological maturity of what they are growing. I'm not sure anyone knows yet what this new breed of leader will look like, but again the mixed ecology provides a place for this model to be embraced, nurtured and amplified.

Talking point

I was keen to find out what my conversation partners, Hannah Steele, Simon Goddard and Jonnie Parkin, thought about how different leaders can view one another across the mixed ecology. I asked them, 'What does a 'generous orthodoxy'[5] of leadership look like in a local mixed ecology?'

Hannah: For me, generous orthodoxy is summarised in the Great Commission. First, the orthodoxy is expressed through its Christocentric nature: the disciples are to make more disciples of Jesus, and no one else. There are also ecclesial (church) boundaries around discipleship (expressed in terms of teaching, baptism and obedience). Second, it is a call to generosity in the global and cultural contexts in which disciples are to be made of 'all nations'. The beauty of the orthodox Christian gospel is that it can find a home in any culture in the world. Our task as leaders and stewards of the Great Commission is therefore to continue this apostolic witness of making disciples of Jesus (orthodoxy!) in every new context, culture and time (generosity). This finds its expression in a willingness to learn from one another.

Simon: Generous orthodoxy recognises the beauty of biodiversity in the missional landscape. It seeks the flourishing of every part of the diverse church. It involves believing that there is room for a wide variety of approaches, as well as making space for conversations about accountability that invite and respond well to questions and constructive critique from those who advocate for other models.

Jonnie: We need to have faith in the vitality of the church, that it is God (not we ourselves) who causes it to grow. This means letting go of the desire to control and micromanage outcomes and structures, but being confident that God's Spirit will blow where it wills. This can be messy and a bit wild, but if it is guided by love, God's order will emerge. It is essential to be able to equip and release good indigenous leaders who will be yoked to Christ. Our role as leaders is to support, train, disciple and encourage. Within that, the role of the ordained – those set apart to preside at the church's celebration of the sacraments – should be maintained in a way that honours lay leadership.[6]

It can be helpful, then, to be aware of the leadership ecosystem within a local mixed ecology. This is because knowing what charisms make up an ecology will help us to understand the dynamics of the ministry leadership environment. High proportions of one leadership population, for example, will have an impact on the shape of the local mixed ecology. Or where there are a lot of people gifted at starting things, nothing may get finished (I can say that as a starter!). If leaders recognise and resource one another in their different ways and develop a collective resilience, it will help in building an integrated mixed ecology.

The mixed ecologists

Within the leadership ecosystem there is one type of leadership that is quite specific: that of the mixed ecology minister. In 2021, Ruth Perrin and I published a piece of research, *The Mixed Ecologists*,[7] in which we coined this term to describe people who feel called to lead different expressions of church at the same time.

The goal of this qualitative study was to explore a form of ordained ministry whereby ministers were engaged in pioneering initiatives alongside time-honoured expressions of church. In broader terms, a minister could combine any aspects of the mixed ecology, but as that could involve multiple permutations, we decided to focus our work on pioneering and the parish. The study revealed that the mixed ecology has much to offer the life of the church: it provides wonderful opportunities to connect with people in new ways. There were three key findings:

Firstly, the mixed ecology can grow the missional reach of the parish. Cultivating the engagement of hospitality, generosity, accessibility, relevance, creativity and flexibility are seen as important in growing new things in a mixed ecology. New expressions of church initiated by the existing parish church tend to draw in de-churched and the parish fringe which the time honoured church hasn't managed to do. Fresh expressions can stimulate relational trust and a contextual approach to mission within time honoured church communities which can lead to further initiatives. Although this is not the intention, both expressions can be a missional entry point for people engaging in one and then settling within another. Many mixed ecologies tend to have more than one new expression of church. These fresh expressions tend to be networked with one another along with more traditional parish outreach projects such as food banks or toddler groups which, combined, can prove effective in extending the missional reach of the whole parish.

Secondly, the mixed ecology can reinvigorate the life of the existing church. The research identified a common need to deepen the missional perceptive and personal discipleship of congregation members, challenging introspection and the belief that things don't need to or indeed can't change. As noted earlier in this chapter, where this is achieved there is often an overlap of lay or ordained leadership between different expressions of church. Lay ministry of time-honoured church members is often developed within a mixed ecology and flourishes where a culture of participation with permission to fail is fostered and where the potential of individuals is noticed and supported.

Special occasions such as Christmas or Harvest Festival often see a gathering where everyone within the mixed ecology convenes at the time honoured church. Leaders and members within new expressions of church often regard the time honoured church as 'our church' and it is seen, along with the clergy, as a hub. New expressions of church can shift the perceptions of time honoured congregations by deepening missional thinking. Where fresh expressions use the parish church building as their venue, the rehabilitation of the building as a 'common space' can be seen, e.g. as a café, gallery or concert venue or through the use of outside land. The disruption due to the COVID-19 pandemic was also seen as a pivotal moment to re-evaluate what should stop, what should start and what should be re-founded.

Thirdly, mixed ecology ministry takes time, team and temperament (or tenacity). Having 'a foot in both camps' is demanding and exhausting, but most said they do this out of a passion for everyone in their parish. Mixed ecology ministers are often creative, visionary and persistent; they are innovators, equippers and risk takers, which is to be affirmed and celebrated. The attitude of the time honoured congregation can help or hinder the growth of a mixed ecology; where the latter is the case, 'unblocking' is often needed. The confidence of time honoured congregations was noted as something that can make or break the development of a mixed ecology. Team is key to enable appropriate capacity and to combat the isolation of mixed ecology minsters. It takes time to pioneer new things and also time to change the outlook of time honoured church members where needed. Collaboration and enabling are often effective leadership models.[8]

Mark Powley, Mission Adviser to the Archbishop of York, has offered a helpful reflection on this research:

It highlights the way, in a secular society, the various elements of a mixed ecology – traditional services, new worshipping communities and social action initiatives – interact to help faith grow. As [the research] later points out, 'many are so far from understanding the Christian faith that multiple small steps are what they need to take to begin to grasp the gospel' (p. 30). A mixed ecology provides multiple stepping-points to deeper commitment, with the local parish acting as a 'hub' or 'node' throughout the process.

Occasionally, there's a mention of 'those called' to mixed ecology ministry; but, as is recognised at the end, mixed ecology has now been adopted as an intended norm for the Church of England.[9]

On one level, I agree with Mark: there is a strong drive among many Christian denominations to make the mixed ecology the norm, in the sense that they strive for local ecosystems made up of different expressions of church with varied ministries. However, although the mixed ecology minister is on the rise, or just acknowledged in a way that better fits what has been happening on the ground for many years, there is something specific about this leadership type. Not everyone is called to hold multiple expressions of church or wants to increase the connectivity between them, while keeping them distinct and autonomous.

There is no official definition of a mixed ecology minister, but I would suggest the following:

Those who work out of the legacy of an existing church but who, from there, develop new founding ways of mission and ministry, expanding the growth and reach of the existing church. Starting new things or holding a portfolio of ministry is an important part of their focus, but is held in partnership with legacy responsibilities.

Following on from this, although there could be a number of variations, the charism of a mixed ecology minister could be described in these ways:

Mixed ecology minister

Why?
Primary trait: Legacy Starter
Secondary traits: Developer, Advocate

What?
Primary trait: Time-Honoured, Runner
Secondary traits: Enterprise

How?
Primary trait: Adapter
Secondary traits: Curator

Where?
Primary trait: Citizen Resident
Secondary traits: Citizen Commuter

Launching and landing

If the mixed ecology allows for change and fluidity, in what ways can expressions of church move from one part of the ecosystem to another? Some communities may recognise a need to do things differently but, in reality, all that is needed is an adaptation, with the foundations of their ecclesiology and missiology staying the same. This might happen through learning from one another in the aspiration spiral, as discussed in chapter 3. Other expressions of church, however, may feel the call to a more radical change by altering the shape of their spaces, places and habitat.

A Canadian friend of mine told me a story about his ancestors that showed one way in which radical change can happen. Owing to changing local alliances, they found that their town was in republican territory. Choosing to remain loyal to the crown, they decided to move their whole town up the coast by placing the buildings on wooden rollers. We may not need to move our churches, buildings and communities to a different physical location, but there can be occasions when the approach and methods, the 'what?' and the 'how?', need to change. Rather than stopping everything and starting again from scratch, churches may decide to launch and land.

I live near the sea – in fact a lot of this book has been written in a café right on the beach – and I have often observed its amazing power. I had a go at kitesurfing in the summer and it's a lot harder than it looks. You need to hold the kite in just the right position so that it doesn't drop into the sea or pull you into the water, but the power it has is enormous. The combination of the water and the wind means that those who are really good at it fly above the waves. It's amazing and slightly terrifying to watch. But the conditions have to be just right to kitesurf. You need a strong wind from the right direction – it's all about harnessing its power. We often refer to a change of direction as a 'sea change', a term that comes from the Shakespeare play *The Tempest*, and derives its meaning from the sea giving us another direction.

Craig Williams has a great analogy about the sea that expresses this idea of change, based on his experience of Newport Beach, close to where he lives in California, where there is a double wave known as 'the wedge'. The shore has a steep incline into the water, which changes the dynamics of the waves. The incoming wave hits a jetty and returns out to sea. In doing so it comes into collision with the next incoming wave, and a high and fast wave is created. Hence it is called 'the wedge'. It is a dynamic (and dangerous) place to surf. We've reflected together that, if the first wave represents one way of being church and the second another, then harnessing the power of both expressions to bring movement and change can create a dynamic. This led us to think about the idea of launching and landing, and using the analogy of harnessing the power of the sea to bring change. Launching is about pushing out into deeper water, taking that step to leave the old behind and start something new and unknown. Landing is about riding the wave towards this new way of being. Figure 13 describes this process, which could be a metaphorical or a physical journey.

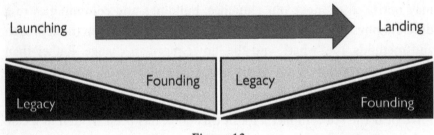

Figure 13

Launching and landing (from legacy to founding)

In this scenario, a legacy church desires to launch and land towards a more 'founding' way of being. This could be a time-honoured church, or an established church plant. The combining forces of legacy and founding can help the leadership and church community to launch and land.

Launching: 'Push out into deeper water'

The analogy of paddleboarding can help us to think through what happens when a church 'launches' or makes a decision to go in a new direction. The incline of the land into the water will affect how easy the launch is. I love to paddleboard, and the beaches where we live have very shallow inclines at certain times of the day. When the tide is out it can take a very long time to get to deeper water, so it takes a lot of energy to launch the board. The best time for launching is at high tide, when the water is a couple of metres deeper and the beach incline drops quickly into the water. The greater the depth of the water, the easier it is to launch, because you can gain momentum quickly. You do, however, have to navigate the shoreline waves before you get to the flatter water.

So, following this analogy, it is better to take the plunge and benefit from the depth beneath your feet. Of course, lots of preparatory work will be needed for this, but in my experience a shallower launching incline just makes it harder. People start to get cold feet and paddle back to shore. The initial shoreline waves that need to be navigated (finances, doubts, opposition, fear of change) can represent the things that might make it harder to launch.

In Figure 13, we can see that the legacy and founding qualities work together to launch the church community from where it currently is, by pushing it out into deeper water. The more fluid waters of the founding quality unlock new potential by accessing the depths of a church's legacy foundations, which act as a base from which to launch.

So what is the legacy land that a church community is launching from? Legacy churches by their very nature will have long-lasting and deep relational roots in the local community. Having been in that space and place for a number of years, they are likely to be made up of Citizen Residents. Most legacy expressions of church will often focus on the cultural fringe. They might effectively reach people who attend church at Christmas and Easter and who come to community and fundraising events hosted by the church.

But there can sometimes be a block on reaching new people and on growing congregations. The cultural fringe is now harder to reach and is thought to be the group that is declining the fastest. Those who are dismissive of church – sometimes called the 'nones', those who reject Christian faith – are growing in number faster than any other group.[10] This means that the methods of missional engagement that churches have relied on in the past are becoming increasingly ineffective.

It might be, however, that churches who focus on community engagement have actually started the founding journey without realising it. The first three stages of the fresh expressions journey, which was explored in chapter 2, are often done instinctively by legacy churches. These stages are: listening, loving and serving, and building community from this. Good examples of this could be a toddler group, a warm-space community drop-in, a social supermarket. Michael Moynagh has often said to me that the process of starting a new Christian community begins with seeing how a group can become a community and how a community can become a church. The process of launching recognises this; however, it can be hard to make it a reality.

This is where the more fluid quality of founding can help. By bringing provocation, innovation and creative cultural engagement, a new perspective and motivation can be given to the things a legacy church already does. The combination of legacy and founding can propel a church community into a new place. It's like the chaordic spaces that were explored in chapter 3, where creative chaos and boundaried order can provide a powerful place for change to happen. One other factor is also at play, namely the wind. When wind moves across the surface of the water, it creates waves. In very general terms, the stronger the wind, the bigger the wave, although there are more complex coastal dynamics at play than this. In the analogy of launching and landing, the wind represents contextual inhabitation, as discussed in chapter 3. This is the process of how known and present a worshipping community is within the local context. The greater the levels of contextual inhabitation, the greater the force that will propel the launch.

Once launched, however, no one wants to bob around in deep water for ever. Being at sea and treading water is exhausting, and being in an ecclesiological and missional limbo isn't good for too long. So when you have launched out from the old habitat, you need a new land.

Landing: 'Riding the wave'

The parish church I grew up in is nearly a thousand years old. The names of the vicars of the church are listed on the wall and go back centuries. It's an indication of the long and valuable journey this church has been on and the many faithful leaders and worshippers who have prayed and worshipped there, which have secured its continued existence. A church such as this brings a wealth of Christian tradition, spirituality, prayer and theological insight that is vital. Think back to the analogy of Brighton seafront and the columns of the West Pier, which still stand tall with strong foundations. Yet this may not be enough to ensure a church's onward growth in a post-Christendom, post-modern world.

When the legacy qualities of a church's ecclesiological and missiological heritage come up against the founding qualities of forming new ways of being church (by making adaptations or more radical innovations or by responding to the missional context), a dynamic movement occurs. The founding quality encourages the emerging missional communities to remain in their context and to ask, 'What would church look like for us in this place?', helping the church to complete its journey. This, combined with the legacy qualities of theological and historical insight and the accumulated wisdom of the church's traditions, gives the church the motivation and power to land and inhabit a new place. The wind of contextual inhabitation also works to propel the worshipping community into its new habitat. Wind also works to mix waters in the sea and, in this analogy, there is often a mixing of the founding and legacy waters at this stage.

Thinking back to 'the wedge', the double wave in California, we could say here too that as the founding wave hits the shore (new ways of being church), it is met by the legacy wave of theological and ecclesiological depth, and the combination creates a bigger wave that lands the expression of church. I think this process might also describe the processes of the Church Revitalization movement. In this model of growth, the intention is to breathe new life into the heart of a dying church, restoring it by building on what was there before, giving it life again.

But it isn't only the legacy churches that might need to change. This process of launching and landing can happen in the other direction too (see Figure 14).

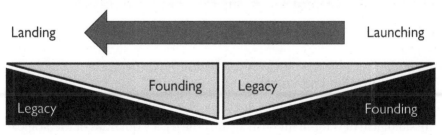

Figure 14

Launching and landing (from founding to legacy)

In this scenario, a founding church – an emerging fresh expression or missional community – desires to launch and land towards a more 'legacy' way of being. Again, the combining forces of legacy and founding can help the leadership and church community to launch and land.

Launching: 'Push out into deeper water'

The founding and legacy qualities work together to launch the church community from where it currently is, pushing it into deeper water. A founding church will have already been responding to the missional context in an attractional or contextual way. In expressions of church that are very founding in their approach, the ecclesiology and structures needed for sustainability can sometimes get lost in the midst of missional innovation. I have noticed that in the training of pioneers over the years, it's very easy only ever to have the experience of starting things. This can happen when the planter or pioneer moves on before the previous initiative is fully formed, either because the leader is called elsewhere or because they have not sufficiently engaged with growing local leadership to continue the development work once they have gone.

Growing something to maturity is a key quality in any leader seeking to start a new Christian community. This is where the quality of legacy comes in – it brings insight into how to hold the cultural and historical story of a community, the role that life events play in deepening a church's roots, and the tried and tested ways of sharing personal faith. This insight can help to launch the founding expression of church into new waters by inspiring it towards a new and more sustainable land. The wind of contextual inhabitation will drive the new Christian community to launch with the motivation of going deeper still into what it is seeking to grow.

Landing: 'Riding the wave'

In this journey, the founding qualities of a church's ecclesiological and missiological development push against the legacy qualities of theological and ecclesial insight. For example, the latter may encompass the role of sacraments in the life of the church, how to foster discipleship well, the patterns and frameworks of worship, insight into governance structures, etc. Drawing on these, the founding qualities of innovation can then explore what they look like as interpreted within the worshipping community. The wind of contextual inhabitation can then propel this landing by driving the worshipping community to a new, more mature habitat that still resonates with the local context.

Finally, it's important to note that some people, especially mixed ecology ministers, will make the journey to and from these different lands on a regular basis. They may well commute back and forth between different expressions of church. These Christian communities may be more static and may not be on the journey themselves, but their leader may make the journey between them. For example, they may be taking a funeral in a parish church in the morning and leading a missional community in the pub in the evening. This will need a lot of energy and a commitment to trying to remain authentic to their different selves in each setting. At times, the launching and landing may feel relatively straightforward. At other times, they may find it harder as they encounter shallow inclines and crashing shoreline waves: perhaps in the form of misunderstanding by those around them. The fact that they are making this journey regularly is something that is important for those around them to recognise, as mixed ecology ministry takes team, time and tenacity. It will also be important for the wider mixed ecology to listen to their adventures, as the mixed ecology minister will probably see more of the distant shores beyond than those who just inhabit one land. Their knowledge, wisdom, stories and insights will be of huge value to all within the mixed ecology leadership ecosystem.

The mixed ecology, then, is a key location for the launching and landing that will deepen and develop the life of many churches. If legacy and founding are to inform each other, leaders and their congregations of different expressions of church within the ecosystem will need to be willing to share their insights, helping others to make their journey. This may be done by engaging with the three principles of mixed ecology or by following a process such as the mixed ecology journey.

Co-creative leadership

Within pioneer circles, the language of 'host and guest' leadership has been used for a while. This seeks to describe two approaches to leadership, one more directive and one more facilitative. In leadership there will be times when different approaches will be needed: in a crisis, clear decision making is required, whereas when trying to communicate a new vision within a community, a more facilitative approach is often best. If integration and connectivity are to grow, however, and if we are to inhabit the three principles of recognition, resourcing and resilience as well as the stages of the mixed ecology journey, we will require both approaches to leadership: in other words, a co-creative leadership. If there are too many host leaders, people will be disempowered, but if there are too many guest leaders, nothing will get done. It is important to get this balance right.

Talking point

To find out what my conversation partners thought, I asked them, 'What does it mean to be a leader who is both a guest and a host?'

Jonnie: Whenever Jesus broke bread, he did so as guest. For a long time the church has invited other people to its own parties. We need to learn how to be guests again, to inhabit other people's spaces and learn their rules and rhythms, and how to share the good news in their space. We need to find the people of peace who can offer us hospitality. We do this as ambassadors of Christ, who is guest but is also the one in whom all things are held together. In host mode we need to be aware of the needs of our guests, putting them at ease and helping them to feel at home in our space, which is in reality God's space, not our own.

Simon: This type of leader recognises that true power is found in the imitation of Christ – in the authority of who Jesus is, and how he lived, died and rose in glory. Being willing to be guest and host requires a letting go of any other source of power or control; it means the willingness to be vulnerable and step into uncomfortable contexts, and to encounter Christ as we let others serve us (as the disciples did when Jesus washed their feet). It also means being willing to step up, to organise, and to lead humbly when this is what God is asking us to do.

Hannah: This will require a willingness to listen to others and see what you might have to learn as well as to offer. It means being attentive to the presence of God already at work in a context, and adopting appropriate prayerful humility in the light of that.[11]

For an integrated mixed ecology to flourish, its leaders will need to work together in a whole variety of different ways. Leaders will bring their own experiences, approaches and priorities. As connectivity grows and becomes more typical across the mixed ecology, the value and presence of co-creating will increase. The leadership qualities of duplication and collaboration are both helpful in developing a co-creating culture.

Growth and loss

Duplication and collaboration can be seen in many aspects of life. This is true in a positive sense that leads to growth, but also in a negative way, leading to loss. Duplication – having multiple amounts the same thing – can bring increased reach; however, too much of the same thing can result in a loss of reserves. Collaboration – working together – can bring a growth of synergy; however, too much can result in a loss of specificity. Duplication promotes working apart in a positive way whereas collaboration promotes working together in a positive way.

The beehive is a good example of this. Duplication brings a growth of reach; the greater the number of worker bees in a colony, the greater the amount of food that can be brought in, which will help the colony to thrive. But if too many hives are located in close proximity (too much duplication), the result will be a loss of reserves, which can harm bees owing to an insufficient food supply and the rapid spread of disease.

Collaboration brings a growth of synergy, as bees collect pollen and nectar from plants to be used as food for the colony and in doing so enable plants to pollinate. But too much collaboration and a loss of specificity can occur. Bee colonies need one queen, drones and workers, each with a specific role. If there is an imbalance of each type and in the interaction between them, the colony may die.

I began exploring the idea of collaboration and duplication a few years ago when I was working on a shared community project. There were a few of us with very similar roles, and at times this was a good thing, but at other times we seemed to get in each other's way. So, with the beehive analogy in mind, I developed 'The Growth Hive', a leadership model to draw out these themes (see Figure 15). This was inspired by a piece of modern art in the Tate Modern, composed of a square with a circle in the middle of it and a diagonal line running from the top left-hand corner to the bottom right-hand side.

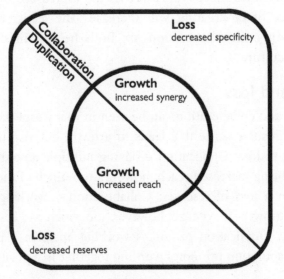

Figure 15

The thinking at the heart of this model is that, for effective co-creative leadership, you need to aim towards growth – positive duplication and collaboration – and away from loss – negative duplication and collaboration.

Growth

Positive duplication can increase the potential for reach:

- By the presence of more than one of the same (or similar) strand, greater presence is achieved across the target landscape.
- By allowing multiple related strands to run in parallel, further depth and detail of each may be found.
- By creating opportunities for specialisms, a more diverse landscape can emerge that can speak to a multi-platform community.

Positive collaboration can increase the potential for synergy:

- By the presence of related but differing strands, a wider perspective can emerge with shared ownership and accountability, which may lead to fruitful partnerships.
- By allowing multiple strands to cohabit and influence one another, their combined value can be greater than their individual parts. Each may become a co-catalyst for the other.
- By creating the opportunity to grow a community of stakeholders, a common vision can be achieved.

Therefore, positive duplication combined with positive collaboration will maximise growth. There may be many ways in which duplication and collaboration can be combined. Sometimes it might be best to first allow duplication to develop and then introduce collaboration to harness the best of the best. At other times, it might be best to start with collaboration and deliver a shared vision through duplicated strands. But if leadership engages in too much duplication and collaboration then loss can begin to occur.

Loss

Duplication can decrease reserves:

- In the presence of overlapping needs, time, resources and energy can be misspent, at the cost of other projects.
- With multiple identical strands running in parallel, motivation can decrease, breeding mistrust and competitiveness.

- When creating opportunities for more of the same, if this is unchecked, a loss of consistency can occur over time.

Collaboration can decrease specificity:

- By the presence of participation in related strands that don't add value to one another, focus can be blurred.
- By allowing multiple strands to cohabit, a common denominator can emerge that can deplete complementary values and constrain creativity.
- In creating opportunities for conflicting strands to interact, the project's purpose can be lost.

It's amazing how easy it is to slip into negative duplication and collaboration. I was talking to someone recently who was overseeing a united benefice containing a number of churches. Two of the churches had a passion for mission on urban estates and for outreach to families. In many ways this is great, as the harvest is plentiful and the workers are few; however, the leadership ecosystem of the united benefice staff team was such that it actually made things less effective. Two of the churches set up 'community hubs' (places for local people to get to know one another) close by in different parts of the same town; both were drawing on the same existing congregation members to help, both were attempting to set up an outreach project to reach young families on these estates. When they realised this wasn't working and decided to work together, the attempted amalgamation of the two projects didn't have a clear and united focus and things became ineffective and began to unravel. If they had given some thought to the positive use of duplication and collaboration to start with, their co-creating would have been more effective. This does, however, rely on leaders intending to work together in the first place.

Theological reflection: The feeding of the 5,000

To return again to the feeding of the 5,000: in the narrative of this miracle, Jesus uses both positive duplication and positive collaboration. Duplication is seen in the twelve baskets, and in the repeated instructions to gather the crumbs and redistribute. Jesus works with what is there. The same baskets and the same bread and fish couldn't feed 5,000 people, but Jesus' miraculous multiplication duplicates the food. Collaboration is seen when Jesus asks, 'Who has any food?' He collaborates with heaven by breaking and giving thanks for the food. He gives instructions to the disciples, who work with him despite their doubts. The crowd also collaborate with the disciples by taking part in the sharing and consumption of the food. Jesus could have chosen to listen to the disciples and simply send the people home to find food there. But he chooses to collaborate rather than work alone. By using the disciples in this miracle he not only reveals more to them of who he is, but also demonstrates the reality of God's power working through them and in doing so trains them for their own future ministry. Duplication and collaboration work together to enable this miracle of growth and multiplication.

Ascension and Pentecost

At the ascension we see a sign of collaboration. The Great Commission in Matthew 28 that precedes Jesus' return to heaven establishes a principle of collaboration by inviting the disciples and those with whom they share their faith to continue the work of Jesus, in partnership with him. To be disciples who make disciples is a mark of collaboration.

At Pentecost we see a sign of duplication through the coming of the Holy Spirit. There is a duplication of languages spoken by the disciples, duplication of the same Spirit of God in each believer, and thus duplication of the number of followers and disciples who make disciples. Ascension + Pentecost = kingdom growth!

Co-creating journey

Co-creating, then, is important in growing an integrated mixed ecology. But this can take time; some groundwork may first be needed. The relationship between *personal autonomy* – self-governance, freedom from external control or influence and independence – and *collective ownership* – shared possession, tenure and maintenance – is the key. As personal autonomy decreases, co-ownership tends to increase.

To enable co-creating, there may need to be a journey from participation to partnership. It may be that co-creating first needs to be grown out of seeking ways to participate, where one party is invited or contracted in for a specific task. In this scenario, personal autonomy is high and collective ownership is low. The individual leader may be accountable for an aspect of the work but doesn't hold overall responsibility. Participation can therefore be an inroad into co-creating.

Once co-creation is present, responsibility for the work may increase and personal autonomy may decrease. Partnership then can be a journey beyond co-creation, where responsibilities are equal or shared. In this scenario, personal autonomy is low and collective ownership is high. Therefore, participation can be a building block for collaboration and collaboration can build partnership. Last but not least, it's important to recognise the perspectives of those engaged in the work, as they may vary. One leader may feel they are a 'participant', whereas another may feel they are in 'partnership'. Clarification of perspective from all involved is therefore the key to managing appropriate expectations and fostering a shared purpose within the mixed ecology.

We have seen that leadership within the mixed ecology is by its nature varied and mixed. There are leadership systems within systems and complex dynamics to navigate. Understanding the make-up of each other's charisms will help with relationships and with defining the leadership potential of the local mixed ecology. This will create a greater possibility for support between leaders, especially if expressions of church are seeking to launch and land. Co-creating will then be more plausible as leadership connections begin to form and flourish.

Questions for discussion

1 How would you describe your leadership charism? How will knowing this help you to gain more insight into your vocation leadership and ministry?
2 Would you describe yourself as a mixed ecology minister? If so, what makes you think that you are? How could this be an important part of developing your leadership?
3 Do you have a desire to launch and land with your worshipping community? How might you go about starting this process?

4 How easy do you find it to co-create with others? Do you keep all the toys, or just want everyone else to be happy? How could thinking about collaboration and duplication help you to work better with others?

Contributors

Jonnie Parkin is Canon Missioner of Bristol Cathedral and is a pioneer.

Hannah Steele is Director of St Mellitus College in London and is a lecturer in missiology, on evangelism and contextual mission.

Simon Goddard is Director of RiverTree, an organisation that he set up in 2018 to catalyse, cultivate and collaborate, to enable fruitfulness in the mission of God.

5

Shaping a mixed ecology

For growth to happen in the mixed ecology, there needs to be an intention to grow. The principles of recognition, resourcing and resilience and the stages of the mixed ecology journey will be actively working only if those involved have the desire to form an integrated ecosystem. Therefore, defining and committing to a vision for the mixed ecology will be needed in order for it to become a reality. This needs to be a community undertaking, as one person cannot do it alone: creating and sharing a vision for the mixed ecology of church must be a corporate effort. In this chapter, I will explore this communal commitment to growing the mixed ecology by using the analogy of a nature reserve, looking at what needs to happen and the roles played by different agents.

Shaping a vision

Nature reserves are really important for maintaining biodiversity in the natural world, especially where this is threatened in some way. The designated space gives protection to the organisms that are already there and also allows for wild things to grow, with some gentle management. We see this at work on a small scale, such as in a piece of land in an urban environment, and on a large scale, such as in our national parks. The idea of a reserve is a helpful model for shaping a vision for a mixed ecology using the five aspects of seeds, a boundary, bees, a hive and existing and emerging organisms (see Figure 16).

Steve Aisthorpe's book *Rewilding the Church*[1] is based on the ecological idea that, in the management of landscapes, natural forces rather than management by humans should be allowed to take the driving seat. Key species may be reintroduced and 'invasive species', which hinder its

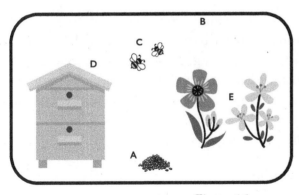

A **Seeds:** new ideas are scattered to cast a new vision.
B **Reserve boundary:** *resilience* in the form of a designated space protected from established ways and means.
C **Bees:** *recognition* of the old and the new. Cross-pollinating of ideas, propagation and promoting growth.
D **Reserve hive:** *resource* provision of support to enable change, formation and guidance.
E **Organisms:** expressions of church and missional communities growing within the mixed ecology.

Figure 16

healthy development, may be monitored or removed. The 'rewilding' of the church, therefore, is about stepping back and allowing the missio Dei to flow freely.

> Rewilding the church argues that our appetite to plan, manage, contain and control has not only led to an environmental crisis, but has also disrupted the natural patterns in the church. The same human instincts that have disrupted our natural environment have also constrained the church. What began as a Spirit-empowered movement has become hindered by excessively complex and risk-averse institutions. The Christian way has been domesticated and it's time to rediscover the adventure of faith.[2]

The book also argues for the value of God rewilding us as individuals. Our inhabiting of a new vision for an integrated mixed ecology therefore derives first of all from a journey of rewilding within ourselves, letting go of even the best-made plans and immersing ourselves fully in God and in the spiritual habitats that lie within us. In shaping a new collective vision for the church, whether on a local or a national scale, there is a need for a season of stepping back and listening to the prophetic voice of God. Things may come to light that need repentance and lament, but there will also probably be valuable insights and experiences brought by different expressions of church, which could be important in reshaping a church of mission.

Drawing on the analogy of the nature reserve, we will explore four aspects of shaping a vision for the mixed ecology of church: casting a vision, supporting a vision, embedding a vision and implementing a vision. As with much that has been explored in this book, it's important to say that these aspects of shaping a vision work as an ecosystem and may happen in a different order and at different times, while in some cases different roles will be held by the same people.

Casting a vision (seeds)

In the analogy of a nature reserve, the seeds represent the people who cast a new vision of a mixed ecology. The purpose of the visionaries is to discern, to be prophetic and to bring the message from the edges. Most new ideas come from the edges of society or in unexpected moments and start small. For example, in 1934 British inventor Percy Shaw saw the reflection of his car's headlights in the eyes of his cat, which inspired him to create the reflective studs in the middle of the road now called cats' eyes.[3] Branding design expert Paul Bennett talks about trying to solve small, overlooked problems by seeing things afresh.[4] Often, these ideas or 'seeds' are initially dismissed by the majority, as they can't make sense of them or find that they challenge the status quo too much. For example, we have known for decades that global warming is a serious problem, yet it is only now, with the increase in wildfires, flooding and extreme summer air temperatures, that its true impact is hitting home. To have taken it seriously before would have meant changing our lifestyles and priorities for no perceived immediate benefit. Faced with the inevitable evidence, we have now started to listen.

The Bible has many seed narratives; the one I find the most engaging is the parable of the mustard seed. One of the shortest parables that Jesus told, it is found in the Gospels of Matthew, Mark and Luke. In Matthew 13:31–2 (NIV, adapted) we read:

He told them another parable: 'The kingdom of heaven is like a mustard seed, which a farmer took and planted in their field. Though it is the smallest of all seeds, yet when it grows, it is the largest of garden plants and becomes a tree, so that the birds come and perch in its branches.'

We have mustard seeds in a jar in our kitchen. The Gospel writers are right: they are really small. If you drop them on the counter or on the floor, they are hard to find and even harder to pick up. Jesus is using hyperbole here, as he so often does. In reality, there are seeds smaller than mustard seeds and shrubs larger than mustard plants, but the point being made is that this seed, which is likened to the kingdom of heaven, produces something big out of something small.

Like the mustard plant, the kingdom of God started with only a handful of believers and grew into a huge community of people. The seeds that visionaries bring may seem small and insignificant and can get overlooked, but in reality they may be the key to growing something of significance.

In 1 Corinthians 12 we read about five revelatory gifts from the Holy Spirit: wisdom, knowledge/revelation, prophecy, discernment and the interpretation of tongues (the other four gifts are faith, healing, miracles and speaking in tongues). The visionary brings divine insight that supports the wider body of the church, and with it the potential for new things to grow.

Much could be said about prophetic leadership, but the following list of descriptions of a prophetic leader is a helpful summary:

- They are trusted and known for having a prophetic ministry;
- They minister and steward words, both for individuals and for the corporate church;
- They are responsible for building a prophetic culture in which the spoken word of God is respected and is used to bring change;
- They steward well the responsibility/ability to lead, shadow and equip people;
- They have a governmental function;
- They call other people's gifts and callings into being;
- They are firmly connected to other prophetic streams/prophetic groups for accountability, testing and the sharpening of one another.[5]

A visionary, then, calls out from the edges, offering fresh insight and casting a way of thinking, but they are not a lone ranger or a maverick; they are part of the body of the church: known, trusted, respected and therefore accountable to others in the mixed ecology. They are part of the leadership ecosystem, helping to make decisions and form the essence of the vision. Like the Old Testament prophets, they are not fortune tellers but rather proclaimers, God's representatives to the people, bringing words of assurance and promise as well as confrontation and warning.[5] They are prayerful, showing God's heart and his intentions for his people.

This can be a hard place to be. Jonny Baker, Britain Hub mission director for CMS, often speaks about 'the gift of not fitting in'.[7] Often, those who are forging new ideas find themselves at odds with established ways of doing things. They are aware that they approach life differently and don't have the same priorities as others. They may have different life experiences and make different choices. As someone who also doesn't always fit in, I have found that it's better to embrace this and see it as a gift rather than as something to be overcome. God needs people who are different; new insights and approaches are much needed in the church today. As the church has increasingly sought to welcome new thinking, the visionary's position has become slightly easier to occupy. I don't think I would ever want to totally fit in now, as I know that my calling is different; I have chosen to embrace this gift.

The role of the visionary isn't just about pointing to what is new. They also have a key role in helping others to identify it. I used to read the story of *Mr Tiger Goes Wild*[8] to my children when they were younger. It's about a tiger who lives in a fairly conventional town, with lots of other animals. They all wear rigid-looking Victorian clothes, walk on their hind legs and uphold polite society. Mr Tiger, however, finds this increasingly frustrating, and one day he decides to take off all his clothes (he is wearing his fur, so that's OK) and walk on all fours, and he starts to swim in the fountain in the park. As a result of various interactions with other, less free-and-easy town animals, he decides to go into the wild to find his roar. After a while he gets lonely, and decides to go back to the town. Again through a series of encounters, the town animals come to see his way of thinking and also decide to take off their clothes (again fur is being worn!) and walk on all fours. On the last page we see the animals in their new way of life; my son would always ask, 'But why are they still wearing their hats?' I was never sure why that was. It might be that they decided to keep some of the good things from their old way of life, that they didn't want to fully make the change or that it was a town with a permanent cold front where heads got particularly cold. We will never know. Mr Tiger is a good example of a visionary. These people are gifted in being able to see what is needed before others can.

There is debate over where the phrase 'With great power comes great responsibility' comes from. Some link it to a version of this phrase written by the eighteenth-century French philosopher Voltaire and some to the 1962 Marvel comic character Spider-Man.[9] Jesus said, 'From everyone who has been given much, much will be demanded; and from the one who has been entrusted with much, much more will be asked' (Luke 12:48, NIV). Visionaries, then, have a big responsibility to pray, to hear clearly from God and to share this in the most appropriate way.

So what are visionaries like and where can they be found in the mixed ecology? I'm reminded of Cathy, someone I worked alongside in Cambridgeshire. She was a member of a church that was part of a group in the East Anglian Fens. She had an instinct for what God was up to, and was passionate about sharing this. She had been part of her local community and church congregation for many years and was respected by the people she knew. She sometimes spoke of feeling as if she were 'working undercover', as she was part of the established form of church but could also see the potential for new ways and was discerning how and with whom she shared this. When she did share, there was always passion in her voice and in her eyes. This wasn't always received favourably, and I know that she was identified as an agitator, someone who would shake things up, which at times made her unpopular in PCC meetings. These meetings were uncomfortable for her, as she felt restricted and boxed in, but she served in this way because she felt God was asking her to. Over time, she discovered who would listen and who could help her to unpack her vision for the local church communities. So, although visionaries are to be found on the edges of the mixed ecology and although they plant seeds that promote the vision of connectivity, they may also quite likely be living among everyone else. Their edginess is in their attitude and outlook – it's not to be found in their living life as a hermit in a remote cottage. To be heard, visionaries need to be Citizens, but could be Residents or Commuters. So try to find a Cathy when shaping a vision or a mixed ecology of church.

Supporting a vision (reserve boundary)

In the analogy of a nature reserve, the boundary represents the people who support the emerging vision of a mixed ecology. As with nature reserves, there is a clear boundary that acts to protect the space within, allowing established and new things to grow in their own way and with freedom from overmanagement. A reserve boundary around a mixed ecology of church enables time for the vision to form, gives recognition to the value of what is emerging, and supports the right expectations.

The purpose of supporters in the formation of a new vision is to provide finance, prayer, resources and support, and to hold all involved to account. These people may or may not be directly involved in the work of casting a vision or implementing it, but are essential to getting things done. I remember doing an evening class in graphic design a few years ago. The person who ran the design company said that the only person who was good at organisation and detail was the administrator; all the others were creatives and big thinkers. Without the administrator, their business just wouldn't work, despite having some brilliant designers creating some amazing things. If you are a big-picture person, it may seem quite frustrating to have to think about the detail of how this thing will be paid for or resourced. It is also easy to get lost in the realms of what could be possible, rather than the reality of what is actually achievable.

Without the appropriate support, the big idea is less likely to see the light of day. Supporters also need to be in place early on when forming a vision. It's important to have people who act as a sounding board. They need to catch enough of the big idea, or trust the person who has it, in order to support it. As in the nature reserve, supporters may also have a role in protecting and defending the beginnings of an idea or fledgling connectivity. These ideas will still be forming and, like wild flowers, will be fragile and self-seeding. Visionaries, advocates and practitioners will often benefit from personal affirmation of their ministry.

To set up a reserve, those involved should agree what the boundaries will be: what is within its scope and what isn't; what will be recognised and resourced for the vision to flourish; and what won't be needed. In many ways, this discussion of boundaries reminds me of my first experience as a stage manager at the community pantomime that we put on in our village last year. I'd been involved in theatre in various ways over the years, but never as a stage manager. The rule in theatre is that the director is in charge during rehearsals and at pre-show warm-up, but as soon as the show starts, the stage manager is in charge. Mostly it involves making sure that everyone and everything is on the stage at the right time, co-ordinating the stage crew and calling the cast to the stage when they are needed. This particular pantomime was the first in our village for a very long time. For various reasons, timings were tight, which meant that the first time the stage crew and actors could run the show on the stage was at the opening performance. This was slightly stressful, as it was a very small stage and there were a lot of people, set and props involved. It went well and was a great success, but afterwards one of the actors said to me, 'Thank you; you knew what was happening next and were so good at keeping us all calm.'

I have no desire to be on the stage, but I love to be involved behind the scenes and get a real sense of satisfaction in seeing everything come together, in solving problems at speed when things don't go to plan, and in supporting the roles of everyone else. The script, the blocking (the agreed places on the stage where actors stand), the technical directions and so forth act as the boundary that gives the freedom for everything to happen. Panto is renowned for a bit of ad-libbing, and this works best when it lies within the general framework of the story and the script. In my experience, actors and stage crew feel safe when they know what's coming next, and where there are clear expectations of what is going to happen if things don't go to plan. The more actors and crew are detached from the plan, the more stressed and confused everyone is. The more there are clear boundaries, the happier everyone is. This may feel counter-cultural, but as humans we actually feel safer when there are clear boundaries, when we and our neighbours know who owns the fences between our respective gardens, for example. We feel safer when we turn up to a social event and know the conventions, or when we have a job interview and have a good idea of what we will be asked. It's the same with casting a vision: when the remit is clear, the vison will be clear too. So setting a clear boundary around vision casting will help it to shape and grow.

So what are supporters like and where can they be found in the mixed ecology? I'm reminded of Steve, who was one of my churchwardens in London. He was one of the most supportive people I have met. I would come up with too many big and unachievable ideas and he would listen and just say, '...OK?!' with a smile on his face. He could see the passion behind the idea but was brilliant at honing it with me, making it into something that was achievable. Having said that, if we decided that we wanted to turn the church into a snowy wonderland for our holiday club, two days later a snow machine would arrive. When we decided to put on a live nativity with actors and animals, he built a stage and organised lighting. To shape a vision for a mixed ecology, supporters will be people who may or may not be directly involved in the day-to-day work of growing connectivity, but they will always give support, guidance, accountability, encouragement and, at times, permission when needed. They might be Citizen Residents within the mixed ecology, but they cbuld equally be Incomer Commuters. They could be overseers within institutional structures or critical friends from beyond the ecosystem. So try to find a Steve when shaping a vision for a mixed ecology of church.

Embedding a vision (bees and hives)

It's one thing to have a great vision for an integrated mixed ecology and people to help make it happen, but quite another when the people in the ecosystem aren't on board. For this to happen, the presence of advocators is essential. These are people who can influence and also facilitate the vision in such a way that people can see its value and want to be part of it.

Propagation

A key feature of a natural ecosystem is propagation, the process by which organisms increase in number. It is useful here to consider the propagation of plants – this can happen in a number of ways, as we will explore shortly. But propagation is also the act of spreading a concept, ideology or piece of information into new places. Social media uses the process of propagation as a mechanism that underpins its connectivity, by means of the Like and Share functions. For a vision of a mixed ecology to grow and spread, propagation will be needed. Pollination, dispersal and runners will all be helpful ways of advocating for the vision of a mixed ecology.

Pollination is the action of pollen grains being moved from the anther to the stigma, which fertilises the plant and stimulates the production of seeds. Cross-pollination or cross-fertilisation is where pollen grains are taken from one plant to another, either of the same species or of another species, which will generate a new variety. This is most commonly done by bees, insects and ants moving from plant to plant. Similarly, influencers and facilitators can propagate a new vision by making connections within expressions of church, linking things that can produce the seeds that give rise to a new way of thinking.

Dispersal is the action of seeds being moved to a different place within the ecosystem by an external force. This might be by airborne seeds blown by the wind, acorns moved by a squirrel or seeds moved by an animal when they become temporarily attached to its fur. In this way, influencers and facilitators can propagate a new vision for the mixed ecology by making connections between expressions of church and missional communities. Dispersal is needed for the vision to flow into new corners of the ecosystem rather than being focused in isolated pockets.

Runners are roots that grow horizontally across or under the soil to clone a new plant from the existing one. Propagation happens when the plant sends out a stem known as a 'stolon', which allows roots to grow into the soil. It also allows vertical or aerial branches to form at specific new points called nodes.[10] An example of this type of plant is a strawberry plant. This process of propagation allows influencers and facilitators to embed a new vision of the mixed ecology by duplicating the vision in multiple places.

Advocate influencers (bees)

In the analogy of a nature reserve, the bees represent the people who cross-pollinate ideas and promote the growth of the vision. They are often embedded in the local mixed ecology as leaders, church members or people within the existing structures, and are likely to be practitioners too. Unlike the visionaries, they may not be at the forefront of the vision casting, but will certainly adopt it early on. They will be people whom others listen to and follow. They will often hold an advocacy role within the local context, bringing thoughts, ideas and research into the local leadership ecosystem and supporting practitioners who want to know more.

Talking point

To find out what my conversation partners, Eddie Green, Alison Myers and Richard Passmore, thought about this, I asked them, 'How important are "advocate influencers" in shaping a local mixed ecology?'

Eddie: Advocates are vital in communicating the possibilities of a mixed ecology in a local context, but also in reassuring people and responding to anxiety. Confidence in speaking of different approaches as *fully church and fully valued* is especially important, both publicly and in more private spaces. Advocates need to inhabit both a prophetic and an evangelistic space, drawing attention to where new expressions of church could potentially be emerging as well as identifying and encouraging future leaders. Many churches have activities that, with support and listening, could become church in their own right, growing alongside new fresh expressions and established forms of church. At All Saints we formally recognised many midweek activities as church in their own right, and adopted the language of *all* our expressions, including Sundays, in our efforts to become more fully church. We also looked at the relationships between the different expressions – for example, a regular BCP Communion attendee would bring their adult children and grandchildren to our midweek preschooler and carers service. We encouraged these relationships across expressions and these people too became advocates.

Alison: They are vital, and their work of advocacy and influence must be continual because, in developing an ecology that gives validity to the emerging expressions of church, we are being counter-cultural; the traditional parish church model has huge centripetal force. Developing a mixed ecology is a culture-changing project. Any such project requires not just advocates and influencers but also role models, heroes and stories that are told and retold. The most powerful influencers and advocates are credible, local people, who are trusted by others who hold power and influence in the existing church communities, whether lay or ordained. If advocates leave an ecosystem before the culture change has reached a tipping point, things can gradually revert to the old ways, pulled back by that centripetal force that is the parish church.

Richard: We also need people in positions of authority to give space and advocate for new things. One of the blocks to mission is a lack of imagination, so advocating and telling stories of creative missional approaches is one of the most effective ways of building towards and influencing change.[11]

Influencers are people who guide, direct and move the vision forward as advocates and promoters. When this happens, it becomes possible to recognise both existing organisms within the ecosystem and the new things that are emerging. Influencers not only share a vision of 'what?' and 'how?' but, more importantly, share ideas about the 'why?' and – in a similar way to the visionaries – will be gifted in spiritual wisdom, knowledge/revelation, prophecy, discernment and interpretation. We will look at change management in relation to advocate facilitators, but the 'why?' is crucial if people are to adopt a new approach. If this is clear, any change – particularly one that involves aspects of loss and sacrifice – can be accepted and enabled.

We recently moved to the south coast of England. We loved where we lived before, and in some ways I still miss our previous home, but it was helpful that the 'why?' was very clear in our decision making. There were all sorts of practical reasons for our move: we can afford to buy what we need down here; we love living by the sea and we're closer to family; but the biggest reason was that through some very focused and miraculous prayer we know that God has called us to put down roots in this area. This has involved change and loss in our friendships, the children have had to move from the school where they were settled, my commute to London is longer, but this is all helped by being clear about the 'why?'. I feel that we have been called to pioneer some new things here. God seems to be calling a number of Christians to the housing development we have moved to. But the rest is yet to unfold.

Influencers have a similar mindset to innovators. They might act on the basis of the following characteristics: divergent thinking, insatiable curiosity, unrelenting stamina, compelling leadership, respect for other innovators and courage.[12] In doing so, they are like bees, sharing the vision with those around them, allowing it to be propagated throughout the ecosystem. Sarah, one of our ordinands at St Mellitus, is a beekeeper. During a lecture I was giving recently, she shared the wonderful analogy of bees as a way of thinking about interconnectedness. She explained that bees live in colonies and roam back and forth from the hive. But what I didn't know is that they leave messages in the wax of the hive about where pollen can be found. Apparently, worker bees, who leave the colony to find pollen, can fly about a mile's radius from the hive and live only for between six weeks and five months, depending on the time of year. This means that, as the old worker bees die, other bees need to know where to find the pollen, hence the messages. Influencer advocates should also leave messages about their vision for the ecclesial and missional communities as they fly back and forth.

So what are advocate influencers like, and where can they be found in the mixed ecology? I'm reminded of a friend of mine called Joel, who is an entrepreneur. He has an amazing ability to get to know many people and is very gifted at seeing connections between them that will be beneficial. As a networker he has great memory recall, which enables him to make these connections, but all of the networking and idea sharing isn't to boost his own ego and to develop the project he is working on, it's for the genuine betterment of others. I've known other networkers and advocates who are all about just scooping up what they can, ultimately to serve their own purposes. The advocate influencer in the mixed ecology of church will be someone who is well connected with many people across different expressions of church and missional communities. They may be Citizens but will probably be Commuters who move around from place to place in bee-like fashion. The messages they leave will be inspired thoughts on the value of the integrated mixed ecology of church and why it is needed. Try to find a Joel when shaping a vision for a mixed ecology of church.

Advocate facilitators (the hive)

In the analogy of a nature reserve, the hive represents the facilitators – the people who help to bring the vision to life in the local context by providing what it needs to grow. The role of the facilitator in some ways is a hybrid of the supporter and the advocate influencer. They are important in the shaping of a vision for the mixed ecology as they take it from the edges (the 'why?') and support leaders and congregations of different worshipping communities in making it a reality (the 'what?' and 'how?'). Another analogy is helpful here – making fudge.

We used to live near Cambridge and we loved going to the fudge shop on King's Parade. It is one of those places where the fudge is made in front of you in the shop. They pour the sugar mix on to a marble table, which has square rods or bars that stop the mixture from dribbling off the sides. Then, using wooden paddles, they fold the fudge in on top of itself until it begins to solidify, before finally cutting it into bite-sized chunks. The folding-in process is needed for several reasons, first of all to cool the mixture so it can solidify and, second, to break down the sugar crystals. This makes the fudge much smoother and nicer to eat.

As I watched this, I was always struck by how the action of 'folding in' worked. It has proved to be a helpful concept for illustrating the process of developing a vision. It brings the emerging vision that happens at the edges (people, ideas, networks) into the centre and also brings the centre to the edges through facilitation, coaching, resourcing and keeping the vision functioning in practical ways. I have found myself in the role of a facilitator fairly often in my working life – it was also part of my job of propagating the idea of the mixed ecology within the Church of England. Part of my task in the national church was to keep an ear to the ground to see what new things were happening within local churches. I did this by drawing on my own experiences as well as those of diocesan advisers and advocates, who could share stories of the things that were happening in their geographical areas. In parallel with and inspired by this, I commissioned research that led to an article in the *Church Times*, wrote more articles, taught about my work in theological colleges, and spoke at mainstream conferences and at diocesan training days. The key was to mix the new ideas on the edge into the established thinking at the centre, using the channels and platforms of the established network while bringing the strategy and priorities of the institution to the edges.

As an innovator and someone who is neurodivergent, I often have ideas that make perfect sense to me but leave everyone else feeling cold or just totally confused. I've found there are things I can see that others can't at first. The things I understand in my own head need some explaining. I'm not saying this to brag, but I started talking about the mixed ecology of church about ten years ago. I remember offering to speak at conferences or host webinars on this subject and not getting much interest or buy-in. A small group of us would talk in coffee shops, in the breaks at gatherings and on train journeys about the need to acknowledge different types of church and to explore the relationship between them, but it never went further than that. Ten years on it's a key part of the agenda, perhaps because the decline in the institutional churches, not helped by the Covid-19 pandemic, means that there is a more immediate need to think in this way.

The main thing for advocate facilitators (and influencers too), therefore, is that they need to be translators of the vision brought by the visionaries.

This means that what is heard and seen can be tested and communicated in a way that is accessible for all. This will help visionaries to hold firm to their message while people catch up. Being ahead of the curve sounds like an arrogant place to be when in fact it is mostly a lonely and frustrating one. Facilitators are enablers of others and will draw on the model of enabling others in leadership, a topic we explored in chapter 4. They will be servant-hearted, often pastors and intercessors with a ministry behind the scenes.

Another key aspect of the role of advocate facilitators is to manage change. When new ideas are introduced, people in the local context can often be anxious about change. For all the benefits an integrated mixed ecology will bring, change and loss will also be inevitable parts of the outworking of the vision. Expressions of church may need to give up exclusive notions of 'the right ways of doing things', or ideas such as 'we can go it alone'. The vision of connectivity may challenge and strain relationships. It may mean that those involved need to adapt the way they relate to one another.

In her book *More Change*, Sarah Yardley writes:

> Every change is marked by some measure of loss. Indeed Rolheiser (1999) reminds us, 'every choice is a thousand renunciations. To choose one thing is to turn one's back on many others. We navigate loss with the things that we choose to change and we wrestle with the losses we would never have chosen'.[13]

To navigate change and loss, we need to address how they play out in the culture of the collective ecclesial and missional community: the collective priorities, language and practices of the Christian communities that make up the mixed ecology. John Kotter defines organisational culture as 'group norms of behaviour and the underlying shared values that help keep those norms in place'.[14] For him, it is the actual behaviour and values that form the culture of an organisation. A church may aspire to be an eco-church but if nothing is done that makes a difference to the natural environment, the culture isn't one of being an eco-church. Kotter notes that it is often the founders of the organisation that set the culture – if successful, it is continued and promoted by subsequent people within that community.[15] A new strategy or vision will not succeed if it is at odds with the dominant culture. We tend to protect what we cherish and hold on to what is dear to us, whether or not it will serve the emerging vision.[16]

How, then, do we change the culture? When I was an incumbent, I discussed at PCC how we could help the church congregation and local community to get to know one another better. My first instinct was to throw a party and let people mingle. My very wise lay reader said, 'No; people get to know one another through a project, not a party,' and she was absolutely right. A community clean-up or gardening project turns out to be a much better way for people to connect with one another than throwing some moves on the dance floor. First, this is because chatting while you work is less intense than a face-to-face conversation with the sole purpose of getting to know someone. I find that tricky conversations are often best had in the car or while washing up. Having something else to focus on makes things less intense. Second, when people work together on a project there is a shared interest and a sense of achievement at the end. They benefit from getting involved in something practical that helps them to form relationships, something that supports the local community and is a blessing for all. This is what creates culture change within the mixed ecology, enabling it to embrace the message of the visionaries and adapter/influencers.

Many have written about the theory of change over the decades. Kurt Lewin suggested that change comes about by moving through the three stages of Unfreezing, Changing and Refreezing.[17] John Kotter suggests stages of creating a sense of urgency, building a guiding coalition, forming a strategic vision and initiatives, enlisting a volunteer army, enabling action by removing barriers, generating short-term wins, sustaining acceleration and instituting change.[18] Writing from a more mission-focused perspective, Sam Wells suggests eight ways of 'being with' a community that can also be helpful in changing culture. These are Presence, Attention, Mystery, Delight, Participation, Partnership, Enjoyment and Glory.[19] Church leader and author Nicky Gumbel usefully suggests five Cs: *commanding* Scripture by asking what the Bible can say to this situation; *compelling* the Spirit by asking for guidance and assessing where God is within this change; seeking the *counsel* of the saints by asking what the godly, prayerful people you know say about this; using *common sense* by asking yourself what the pros and cons are; and, finally, looking for *circumstantial signs* by asking if there are any God-incidences in it.[20] These approaches, and others too, when utilised by a facilitator, can help the process of embedding the vision for a new way of being together in the mixed ecology.

Another key to changing culture is the rate of change. Sometimes we are not in control of how fast or slowly things will change. Rapid change will require a strong faith as we hold on to the unchanging promises of God, focusing on what is essential and maintaining a kingdom-shaped perspective. Slow change will require a faith that protects the promises of God, involving a focus on hope and being known by God and others.[21] Change may come quickly, as the vision of a mixed ecology spreads among its inhabitants, or as external factors that are outside the control of the mixed ecology bring change to individuals or groups and communities. This may cause people some frustration – they may feel things are moving too fast and in an uncharted direction. Change may also come slowly as the vision takes time to embed. Expressions of church and missional communities may need time to consider what the future looks like, weighing up what the costs and benefits might be. This may frustrate those who want things to move at a faster pace. The reality is that a vision for change often does take time, and if rushed it won't build lasting roots for the future. There is, however, a tipping point – when enough of the local leaders and local Christians agree to a vison, things can then start to speed up. The role of the facilitators is to enable this process to happen at the appropriate speed for the specific people involved. Forming and deepening relationships through spiritual discernment, listening and conversation will be essential here.

When I trained as a coach with 3D Coaching, I was taught the value of starting and ending a coaching conversion well. At the start of a conversation, it is really useful to help the 'thinker', the person receiving the coaching, to work out and agree what the focus of our time together will be. This means that the conversation has a clear direction. The two key questions I always ask are, 'What would you like to be different at the end of our time together?' followed by, 'And how will you know you have achieved this?' The first question invites the thinker to identify what they would like to gain, for example to find a solution or to know what a next step might be. The second question asks them to articulate how this will move them on in their thinking, for example, if they say, 'I will have increased confidence' or, 'I will know what I need to do and how to do it.' Ending a conversation is also very important. I often revisit the opening question and check to see if we have fulfilled it. I also ask, 'What do you know now that you didn't know when we started?' This means that the work that has been done isn't lost but is focused, giving the thinker something to take away that will make a real difference. Asking good questions is also important for facilitators in the shaping of a vision for a mixed ecology. They will need to listen in an unbiased way, allowing the thinkers (the different expressions of church) to do their own work at the pace that works for them.

So what are advocate facilitators like, and where can they be found in the mixed ecology? I'm reminded of Liz, someone I knew in my curacy. In some ways she was on the edges of leadership and decision making in the life of the church and so could observe the dynamics of individuals and community, but she was also fully embedded in people's lives. She was very good at drawing alongside people at their point of need. She was a great cook and gifted at hospitality, and would often invite people to her home for food and a chat. She was an excellent listener and would always pause before responding to a question, enabling her to offer advice and good counsel that was accessible for people. In this way she straddled the edges and the centre.

The advocate facilitator in the mixed ecology of church will again be someone who is well connected with many people across different expressions of church and missional communities. They may be Citizen Residents – this is essential, as they will need to hold the trust of those around them. They will be able to catch the vision from the visionaries and advocate influencers and be able to 'fold this in' to the expressions of church and missional communities. This may be done from a central point, for example at a tent meeting of leaders and their communities as part of the mixed ecology journey, or on a more local, individual, one-to-one basis. As is the case with the influencers, a good number of facilitators will be needed, ideally located throughout the ecosystem, in order for the vision of a mixed ecology to be folded in. Try to find a Liz when shaping a vision for a mixed ecology of church.

Delivering a vision (organisms)

In the analogy of a nature reserve, the organisms (in this example, plants) represent practitioners, the people who are the lifeblood of the initiative and get the work done. These are the people who are leading and running the different expressions of church and missional communities. Some will have been around for a long time and some will be new. Without them, the mixed ecology would not exist. They actively and consciously start to make connections between the different inhabitants of the ecosystem in order to build connectivity. Living out the principles of recognising, resourcing and resilience within the mixed ecology, they engage with all stages of the journey and experiment in practical ways across different organisms in the ecosystem. They share this ability to break new ground with entrepreneurs as they hold vision and practice together.

The practitioners will need to listen to the visionaries and the advocates. By doing so, they will catch the vision for an integrated mixed ecology. They will need to sit down with the facilitators, who will help them to make a plan based on what they have heard. They will need to talk to the supporters, who will be the means for these plans to become a reality. This will take them on a metaphorical (and perhaps literal) journey from the familiar into new spaces.

Before Jesus ascended to heaven, he gave his disciples the commission to 'be my witnesses in Jerusalem, and in all Judea and Samaria, and to the ends of the earth' (Acts 1:8, NIV). This follows a series of concentric geographical circles, starting with Jerusalem and heading out to the areas of Judea and then Samaria and beyond. There is a sense here that the disciples start with what is known and familiar and gradually move further out into the unknown and less-familiar spaces and places. The 'ends of the earth' also implies that Jesus is calling them to something with an infinite boundary. Most importantly, they are to do this in the power of the Holy Spirit, which will be essential for such a great task.

For practitioners who are living out the vision of a mixed ecology, there is a similar commission to be witnesses to the vision in their own expression of church or missional community, as well as in neighbouring ones, to the ends of the mixed ecology. They will probably start locally in their own expression of church or missional community, helping those with whom they inhabit the space and place to join in the practice. As their vision and practice grow, they can share them further afield. The more practitioners get involved, the further the vision will spread. This has to be a collective movement. Again, this will only happen in the power of the Holy Spirit, who moves the hearts of the people and empowers them for the task ahead. Practitioners will need to be people of faith, willing to step into new territory with Jesus, putting words into action. To do this, they will need to implement the vision, commit to the vision and lead others into the vision.

Implement the vision

Practitioners need to inhabit a vision that is so compelling that they simply have to act on it. Whether this is a vision born in them or caught from a visionary or advocate, they will have a passion for it, and will be motivated to keep going until it becomes reality. My sister lives in the United States, close to Atlanta, Georgia. Last summer we visited her and her family, and while we were there we went to a playground in Alpharetta, near where they live. It was a big structure set in a one-acre plot and made of wood with platforms, sandpits, turrets and raised walkways; great for exploring and running around. There seemed to be nothing out of the ordinary until I noticed a plaque on the front, which said:

> **We built it together**
> Wacky World is dedicated to the community and to the 2,673 volunteers who built it. After a year of planning, the playground was built in 6 days May 4 1997.

Local people donated money, materials and services to build the playground, and the schoolchildren named it Wacky World. Now, twenty-seven years on, they are embarking on a journey to do the same again and to build a new park to replace the existing one.[22] This really took me by surprise. It's an incredible achievement on a colossal scale – a whole community has inhabited and implemented a vision and has brought something unbelievable to life. This collaboration and co-creation are crucial for practitioners who are seeking to implement the vision for the mixed ecology.

Nehemiah was passionate about the welfare of the city of Jerusalem and in particular about rebuilding its walls. His detailed planning enabled him to achieve something remarkable. His heart for the exiled people – we read of the ways in which he helped the poor and needy in Nehemiah chapter 5 – motivated him to make the building of the wall a reality, since he could see what this would achieve. He was able to fend off opposition from Sanballat the Horonite and Tobiah the Ammonite official. There is a detailed account of the many people who were involved in the building and which part of the wall they built (Nehemiah 3). We are not explicitly told whether Nehemiah was personally involved in building the wall, but the fact that he went to inspect the wall himself, his passion for the project and its benefit to the people, and the language of 'Let us start rebuilding' (Nehemiah 2:17–18, NIV) might imply that he was. This emphasis on planning and collaboration shows Nehemiah to be someone who could implement an audacious vision.

Be committed to the vision

Practitioners will need to persist in bringing the vision into reality, because when pioneering anything new there are always obstacles. Not everyone will see the need for an integrated mixed ecology. Not everyone will work at the same rate of change, not everyone will be committed to the mixed ecology journey, not everyone will stay the course and not everyone will be able to find the right resources. Commitment and courage will be needed to keep going.

Mary the mother of Jesus always strikes me as someone who embodied this commitment and courage. We don't know very much about her but what we *do* know, especially from the annunciation narrative in the Gospels, reveals a young woman who was resolutely committed to the call of God despite all the odds. When I was an incumbent in London, we decided to host a digital nativity art exhibition. We created three digital installations that explored different aspects of the birth narrative. One piece, called 'Digital Mary', was a talking portrait of Mary, surrounded by a gilt frame, projected on to the wall of a small screening room. We filmed the piece with an actress who improvised what Mary might have been thinking and feeling. There is a poignant moment when she talks about Joseph's lack of understanding and the scorn she might be faced with from the local community. She looks straight into the camera, pauses and then simply says, 'It's difficult.' She then goes on to reflect on what God has done in her life and her trust in him.

Mary was faithful, prayerful and responsive in her obedience. She was willing to take a risk, persisting despite the prospect of accusation, and endured a gruelling physical, emotional and spiritual journey.

She could do this only because she knew the 'why?': after her encounter with the angel, she grasped that the Messiah was to be born and affirmed her resolve in the words of the Magnificat. Similarly, committing to the vision of an integrated mixed ecology will involve resolve, persistence and knowing your 'why'.

Lead the vision

Practitioners will also need to lead others into this new vision. Visionaries and advocates may inspire early adopters to action, but the majority of people will need something more. In my experience as an innovator, I have found that people need to see something in order to understand it. A small example – it doesn't need to be the finished article – can really help. It can be hard to imagine yourself into an unknown space and place, especially when getting there will involve a level of change. Good leadership will enable this to happen.

I love watching TV shows such as Channel 4's *Grand Designs*, which follow the design and building of homes. In the planning stages, the client whose house it will be often can't imagine the space just by looking at the plans. It's hard to judge how big the rooms will be, what the view will be like from the windows, how their furniture will look when they move in. I know that, when buying our new-build house, we did our best to imagine it from the plans, but we only really knew it was the right house for us after visiting the show home. In a BBC TV design programme called *Your Home Made Perfect*, two designers pitch to transform someone's home. Part of the pitch involves creating a digital model into which the owners step using VR goggles to help them to choose which design they want to go with. What was always amazing was their experience of being 'inside' the VR model. It helped to make what was planned real. Walking around the digital mock-up enabled them to realise which was the right design for them.

Likewise, in living out the vision of a mixed ecology, later adopters will be hugely helped by being able to glimpse some of the reality that is proposed. They won't have VR googles, but meeting practitioners and supporters who are directly involved in the work on the ground and who can share real-life stories will help. It might involve meeting people from a neighbouring integrated mixed ecology with a similar community dynamic, where the vision has already been adopted and put into practice. Or it might mean meeting practitioners from the same emerging mixed ecology who can share what they have been doing in their own corner of the ecosystem, where they have been growing a micro ecology in which a couple of different expressions of church or missional projects are running in parallel or in partnership. Engaging with research and analytical thinking will also help to make sense of the 'why'. The Mixed Ecologists research, for example, reveals the benefits and challenges encountered by real-life practitioners and also advocates for the integrated ecology.

In leading people into the vision for a mixed ecology, however, practitioners (especially passionate ones) will need to stand aside and allow other practitioners to step into this journey. The narrative of Moses crossing the Red Sea gives us a good example of how to lead in this way. Exodus 14:19–21 (NIV) tells us:

> Then the angel of God, who had been travelling in front of Israel's army, withdrew and went behind them. The pillar of cloud also moved from in front and stood behind them, coming between the

armies of Egypt and Israel. Throughout the night the cloud brought darkness to the one side and light to the other; so neither went near the other all night long. Then Moses stretched out his hand over the sea, and all that night the LORD drove the sea back with a strong east wind and turned it into dry land. The waters were divided, and the Israelites went through the sea on dry ground, with a wall of water on their right and on their left.

Moses showed directive leadership by petitioning Pharaoh and leading God's people out of Egypt. He was able to do this because he understood the promise of the land and the power and calling of God. At the key moment of crossing the sea, taking his lead from the angel and the pillar of cloud, Moses stepped aside, moving out of the way to let the Israelites cross as he held his hand out over the water all night. The text doesn't tell us when Moses crossed the sea, but by implication it must have been last, so that the waters could continue to be held back until all had crossed. Practitioners should learn when they need to be directive and when a more facilitative approach is required, as they lead others into the new land of the integrated mixed ecology.

So what are advocate facilitators like, and where can they be found in the mixed ecology? I'm reminded of Jude, a great friend who is very talented at working with children and families. She is someone who gets things done. She thinks big but also thinks practically. I'd say she is the queen of holiday-club planning and organising, coming up with engaging themes, great drama, amazing activities and games. More than this, she is good at gathering teams of people to get involved with what needs to be done. She is an encourager and can spot potential giftings in people. The results speak for themselves, as her ministry with children and families is growing.

A practitioner in the mixed ecology of church will be someone who is a doer, able to catch the vision of integration and connectivity and bring it to life. They will be people who are leading an expression of church or missional community within the mixed ecology from a range of leadership charisms. They could be Citizen Residents or Incomer

Commuters; they may be involved in one expression of church, or may be an overseer of others or a mixed ecology minister. They could be the licensed or appointed leader of a worshipping community or could equally be someone who is part of the team contributing to the life of that expression of church. They will also benefit from being completer-finishers, people who carry out their work to completion. Try to find a Jude when shaping a vision for a mixed ecology of church.

Shaping a vision within institutional structures

We have explored the roles of supporters, visionaries, advocate influencers, facilitators and practitioners as they are vital for shaping a vision for an integrated mixed ecology of church. As noted at the start of this chapter, these roles may be taken by various different people, though in reality several of these tasks may be carried out by the same person. In this sense there is an ecosystem of leadership, which will have its own nuances and dynamics in each mixed ecology. Another key aspect that needs to be considered are the hierarchical structures and power dynamics that are above or that underlie the mixed ecology. This is the case especially within institutional denominations, particularly if the mixed ecology is seeking to be an ecumenical one.

Talking point

To find out what my conversation partners thought about this, I asked them, 'What structures may need to be changed in order for a local mixed ecology to be shaped?'

Alison: There is a fear at all levels that working with a mixed ecology means not working with the parish system. It might be that a benefice-, team- or area-wide BMO (Bishop's Mission Order) would provide a vehicle for governance that would enable new communities to be grown within the community of the benefice/team/area, where a direct link with a particular parish would be problematic, but something new can still exist alongside it. Training needs to address the polarisation whereby ministerial roles are seen either as parish (i.e. time-honoured) or as pioneering/planting and entirely other, and not just practically but theologically. I speak to too many ordinands and curates who feel that their self-concept as a priest will be undermined by growing communities beyond the standard parish model, and that their understanding of incarnational ministry includes a preference for working with a single community, rather than the possibility of multiple communities of different kinds. A theological understanding of a mixed ecology and of developing and ministering within it needs to be extended to laity too via language, sponsorship by senior leaders and the sharing of stories, etc. And those setting up the many deanery- and area-wide planning and collaboration exercises going on across dioceses at the moment need to know how to speak about the mixed ecology. There is an opportunity just now that may not be grasped.

Eddie: If at all possible, those in structural leadership roles also need to be embedded in a typical context so they can speak strategically and from their own practice. This does not mean they have to be in charge in that context. Training and formation need to be practitioner-informed at every level. At All Saints for many years, we had a senior staff member of a theological college who participated in the life of the church, from BCP through to Forest Church. Not only did this inform the teaching and formation of ordinands, but we gained much from their insight and broader view.

Richard: We need all leaders to be trained in adaptive change and in understanding the missional context they are in. We have to develop a culture of releasing and risk taking at all levels, backed up by high accountability, low control and resources. There has to be a shift from hierarchical to collaborative leadership (at all levels), including more flexibility on how stipends and resources are used.[23]

In the 2023 Reith Lectures entitled 'Our Democratic Future', Professor Ben Ansell gave a series of fascinating talks in which he explored the threats to our safety as a society and what we can do to protect ourselves. The second lecture considered the idea of the future of security, addressing how societal and governmental polices seek to control the threats we face. What was most interesting was his exegesis of the experience we have of safety in our everyday lives. He compared our levels of safety at home and in public and the way we change our behaviour accordingly. In the safety of our homes (if they are deemed safe places to be), we will feel comfortable leaving our phones, keys, bank cards and personal items in communal spaces, because we trust those we are living with. In public, by comparison, we will generally consider the environment to be less safe and will be more cautious about keeping such items close to us. So we will lock our homes and cars when we leave them. He went on to say that to increase our feeling of safety in the public domain we have two choices: build trust through cultivating relationships, or decide to trust no one.[24]

Government institutions in the democratic world are there to promote safety and preserve freedoms without dictating what we as a society can and can't do. Professor Ansell went on to explore what exists either side of this: anarchy, where there is no one dominant governmental structure present, and tyranny, where there is an absolute governmental structure. With reference to CCTV, facial recognition and the rules imposed during the Covid-19 pandemic, the lecture questioned how democratic democracy actually is in the Western world.[25]

These themes are relevant to the exploration of power and structure within the shaping of a vision for the mixed ecology. First, if visionaries, supporters, advocates and practitioners emerge and a vision begins to form, there will need to be a democratic framework that holds it together. Where there is too little, anarchy will prevail in which everyone is out for themselves, but where there is too much, tyranny will squash individuality, difference and distinctiveness. To create a proper framework, those within the mixed ecology will need to feel safe. There will probably need to be a metaphorical move from locking their church doors when they go out to feeling safe enough to leave them open. They will make progress as trust is built, which will lead to new relationships forming. This will be achieved by inhabiting the three principles of recognising, resourcing and resilience and by engaging with the mixed ecology journey.

Second, even if the vision of a mixed ecology can be shaped locally, there may also need to be a shaping of the local and national ecclesiological structures that surround it. Such structures can, most obviously, play the role of supporters and facilitators by providing permission to use buildings creatively, offering prayer support and delivering coaching. As noted above, however, for this to happen, the concept and value of a mixed ecology, where different expressions of church and missional communities are growing in connectivity, will need to be embedded within these structures. Some institutions, such as the Church of England, are advocating for this, which is beneficial, but it will need to be accompanied by genuine recognition of the validity of different types of church and their place within the mixed ecology. Evidence for this will be in the national discernment and formation of its leaders, representing a wide variety of leadership charisms, and the appointment of many different types of leader. It will be in the way funding is apportioned across different expressions of church and missional communities as well as the way permissions are granted for the use of buildings. It will also be in the power that is held and the decisions that are made, which should be representative of different expressions within the mixed ecology so that all are heard. Therefore, the visionaries also need to speak into or be embedded in the power structures, where advocates and even practitioners can propagate this vision.

Questions for discussion

1 Who are the supporters, visionaries, influencers, facilitators and practitioners in your local community?
2 Where is there an absence of these roles and what types of people are needed?
3 Think about the work done to identify types of mixed ecology charisms from chapter 4. How does this relate to and have an impact on shaping a vision?

4 What principles from theories of change would help you to 'fold in' a vision for an integrated mixed ecology?

Contributors

Alison Myers is Warden of Launde Abbey. She is the former Team Rector of the Lordsbridge Team, a mixed ecology Team Ministry in the Diocese of Ely.

Richard Passmore is Director of the Northern Mission Centre, overseeing pioneering and Fresh Expressions across Cumbria.

Eddie Green is Vicar of All Saints, Leavesden. He is also Community Enabler and Chair of Sanctum, a sacramental missional network.

Conclusion

The mixed ecology has much to offer the twenty-first-century church. In an increasingly post-Christendom and apostolic cultural climate, the church faces new challenges as it seeks to respond to a changing landscape. It's a task that will be hard for churches and missional communities to face on their own, and therefore collaboration will be increasingly valuable. Those who feel they thrive in this climate will probably be needed to resource others appropriately with their insight and creativity. The growth of connectivity and interdependence will foster integration, which will bring support and challenge where required.

As we have seen, the notion of growing an integrated mixed ecology is something that will take a collective commitment as we recognise the need to work together. Power dynamics will need to shift, leadership patterns will need to adapt, and vision casting will need to be folded in. There will need to be a greater awareness of the spaces and places that Christian communities inhabit and how they resonate with the local missional contexts around them. The fundamental question of 'What is church?' will need to be posed honestly and openly as connectivity grows. Likewise, as Ian Mobsby explored in chapter 2, the theme of reconciliation will be a key foundation stone in building an integrated mixed ecology. Where there are divides between the old and the new, the mainstream and the edges, the big and the small, we may need to engage in a season of lament in order to reach reconciliation.

I'm acutely aware that there aren't many specific examples of integrated ecosystems to draw from. As a result, this book tends to be rather theoretical; however, my hope is that it will inspire more examples to emerge. Someone once told me that in order to influence 'up the ladder' nearer the structural powers that be, you need to share statistics. These people are often gatekeepers, giving out money and permission and, in a narrative of financial scarcity, it can be hard for funds to be released without knowing whether they will be a wise investment. Evidence such as detailed research, wise analysis and numerical growth relating to the benefits of the mixed ecology will be important in enabling more investment to be directed towards growing an integrated church.

To influence people 'down the ladder' nearer the grass roots, the practitioners on the ground, you apparently need to share stories. These people – local church leaders and Christian communities – benefit from being inspired by tales of what could be that address the real questions they are grappling with. How will our church grow? How will we find the resources to do what we feel God is asking us to do and to be? How can we sustain the mission and ministry we are currently doing? How do we respond to a world that seems so different from the one we knew a generation ago? These stories need to be of the everyday as well as of the exceptional.

I did some work for the national Church of England a few years ago to see what kinds of stories would inspire local churches to try to do something new. Up to this point, much of the storytelling, in the pioneer world anyway, was done by innovators launching out-of-the-box expressions of church that wowed those who were listening. But it turned out that although lots of local churches admired these stories, they were actually unhelpful, because they were just too far removed from what most people could perceive or achieve in their own community. What was in fact needed were everyday stories arising from a context that was similar to their own.

We also realised that we told only the final part of these stories: the part where it has all come together, the funding has arrived, the people have turned up and the world has been changed. In reality, what would have been far more useful are stories from the start, where things didn't work first time, where no one came for a while, where funding had to be prayed for. So, in seeking to grow the mixed ecology locally, everyday stories, stories about a vision that is not quite finished – 'We could do that' – will be far more useful.

So, as we reflect on why the mixed ecology is important, and as we think about integrating, inhabiting, leading and shaping a vision for the mixed ecology of church, we do so in anticipation of what is to come. It may well be that the map unfolds as we read it and may not make sense to everyone at this point in time. It will certainly be a journey that will need to keep evolving. For example, we haven't touched on digital and hybrid churches in this book. The Covid-19 pandemic gave rise to digital churches and of course they emerged out of necessity, but it's interesting to see what has remained in the years that have followed. Not everything is still online – I think the majority of in-person congregations returned to being so when they could. But many churches still live stream their services, have kept Zoom prayer groups going, and use WhatsApp as a way of keeping in touch with discipling and missional relationships. There is now a distinction between online church (church that is formed and operates in the online space) and church online (church that is in person in format but is also shown online). This points to a digital and hybrid mixed ecology of church, ecosystems which the themes of this book can also be used to grow.

So is the mixed ecology of church the norm? In some ways, yes, it is, because it describes the mix of expressions of church and missional communities that have always been in existence in their diversity. But is the integrated mixed ecology of church the norm? I think less so, and here is the area the church can focus on as it seeks to be the body of Christ, unified but not uniform. It will take time, team and tenacity but, by both maintaining their distinctness and living in active relationship, different expressions of church and missional communities can benefit the mutual missional and ecclesial kingdom of God.

Notes

Introduction

1 Adapted from *The Blended Church*, unpublished paper, Diocese of Ely, 2016.

2 'Vision and Strategy: A vision and strategy for the Church of England in the 2020s', www.churchofengland.org/about/vision-and-strategy.

3 'Question: What is the rock in Matthew 16:18?' Got Questions: Your Questions, Biblical Answers, https://www.gotquestions.org/upon-this-rock.html.

4 'The Pioneer Spectrum', Pioneer Mission Training, Church Mission Society, 2010–24, https://pioneer.churchmissionsociety.org/pioneer-spectrum/.

5 'A Walk Down Memory Lane: History', https://www.brightonpier.co.uk/history-of-the-pier.

6 Harry Sherrin, 'The Rise and Demise of Britain's Victorian Pleasure Piers', 23 March 2022, https://www.historyhit.com/the-rise-and-demise-of-britains-victorian-pleasure-piers/.

7 'Brighton i360', Marks Barfield Architects, 2024, https://www.brightoni360.co.uk/.

1 Why a mixed ecology?

1 Missio Dei involves, as Rowan Williams put it, 'finding out what God is doing and joining in'.

2 Graham Cray, *Mission-Shaped Church: Church planting and fresh expressions of church in a changing context* (London: Church House Publishing, 2004).

3 Ed Olsworth-Peter, *Mixed Ecology Learning Pathway*, Church of England, unpublished, 2021.

4 Dave Walker, '"Mixed Ecology" Ministry', *Church Times*, 4 June 2021.

5 'The Fresh Expressions Journey', Fresh Expressions, 2022, https://
freshexpressions.org.uk/get-equipped/the-fresh-expressions-journey/.

6 'The Community of St Etheldreda', 20 April 2023, The Church of
England, Diocese of Ely, https://www.elydiocese.org/the-community-
of-st-etheldreada.php.

7 *Mission-Shaped Church*, pp. 32–5.

8 A Latin Christian theological term that can be translated as the
'mission of God' or the 'sending of God'.

9 Jürgen Moltmann, *The Church in the Power of the Spirit: A contribution
to messianic ecclesiology* (Philadelphia, PA: Fortress Press, 1993), p. 64.

10 Michael Moynagh, *Church for Every Context: An introduction to
theology and practice* (London: SCM Press, 2012).

11 Karen Sawrey, *Infographic Bible: Visualising the drama of God's word*
(Glasgow: William Collins, 2018).

12 'Talking Jesus: 2022 Research Report', Evangelical Alliance, Church of
England and Hope Together, 2023, www.talkingjesus.org/research.

13 'Talking Jesus: 2022 Research Report'.

14 Stuart Murray, *Post-Christendom: Church and mission in a strange new
world*, 2nd edn (London: SCM, 2018).

15 Ed Olsworth-Peter, *Mixed Ecology Learning Pathway*, Church of
England, unpublished, 2021.

16 Lesslie Newbigin, *The Gospel in a Pluralist Society* (London: SPCK,
1989), pp. 232–3.

17 Sawrey, *Infographic Bible*, pp. 185–6.

18 'Bishops Set Out Principles for Church Planting', Church of
England, 26 June 2018, www.churchofengland.org/news-and-media/
news-and-statements/bishops-set-out-principles-church-planting.

19 General Synod Paper GS2142, 8 July 2019.

20 Christine Dutton, 'Unpicking Knit and Natter: Researching an
Emerging Christian Community', *Ecclesial Practices* 1, 2014, pp. 31–50.

21 Michael Moynagh, 'Blended Church', unpublished paper, January
2019.

22 George Lings, *Encountering 'The Day of Small Things'* (Sheffield:
Church Army, 2017), p. 117.

23 Lings, *Encountering 'The Day of Small Things'*.

24 'Paid Pioneers: From the margins to the mainstream?' Research Unit,

Church Army, June 2022, https://churcharmy.org/our-work/research/recently-completed-research/paid-pioneers/.

25 'Talking Jesus Research', 2022, www.talkingjesus.org/research. Incidentally, this number has dropped from 68% in the 2015 research.

26 https://pioneer.churchmissionsociety.org/pioneer-spectrum/.

27 Stuart Murray, *Post-Christendom: Church and mission in a strange new world*, 2nd edn (London: SCM, 2018), p. 167.

28 Stuart Murray, *Post-Christendom*, p. 167.

29 Lings, *Encountering 'The Day of Small Things'* (Sheffield: Church Army, 2017).

30 Thomas Merton, *Conjectures of a Guilty Bystander* (New York: Doubleday, 1966), pp. 53, 294–5.

31 Abbot Christopher Jamison, *Finding Happiness: A monk's guide to a fulfilling life* (London: W&N, 2020), pp. 84–6.

32 Harvey C. Kwiyani, *Multicultural Kingdom: Ethnic Diversity, Mission and the Church* (London: SCM, 2020), p. 11.

33 Janet Soskice, *The Kindness of God: Metaphor, Gender, and Religious Language* (Oxford: OUP, 2008), p. 51.

34 Emmanuel Katangole, 'Mission and the Ephesian Moment of World Christianity: Pilgrimages of pain and hope and the economics of eating together', *Mission Studies*, Vol. 29, No. 2, 2012, p. 191.

35 Andrew F. Walls, *The Ephesian Moment: The Cross-Cultural Process in Christian History* (Orbis, NY, Maryknoll 2002), p. 77.

36 Walter Hollenweger in Kwiyani, *Multicultural Kingdom*, p. 54.

37 Reni Eddo-Lodge, *Why I'm No Longer Talking to White People About Race* (London: Bloomsbury, 2018); George Yancy (ed.), *Christology and Whiteness: What Would Jesus Do?* (Abingdon: Routledge, 2012); Afua Hirsch, *Brit(ish): On Race, Identity and Belonging* (London: Penguin, 2018); Ta-Nehisi Coates, *Between the World and Me* (Melbourne: Text Publishing, 2015); Ben Lindsay, *We Need to Talk about Race: Understanding the Black Experience in White Majority Churches* (London: SPCK, 2019); Anthony Reddie, *Is God Colour-Blind? Insights from Black Theology for Christian Faith and Ministry* (London: SPCK, 2010); A.D.A. France-Williams, *Ghost Ship: Institutional racism and the Church of England* (London: SCM, 2020); Robin DiAngelo, *White Fragility: Why It's So Hard for White People to Talk About Racism* (London: Penguin, 2019).

38 Katherine Phillips, 'How Diversity Makes Us Smarter', *Scientific American*, 1 October 2014, https://www.scientificamerican.com/article/how-diversity-makes-us-smarter/, accessed 5 January 2021.

39 Jonny Baker and Cathy Ross, *Imagining Mission with John V. Taylor* (London: SCM 2020), p. 4.

40 George W. Fisher, 'Symbiosis, partnership, and restoration in Mark's parable of the sower', *Theology Today*, 2017.

41 Walter Brueggemann, *The Land: Place as gift, promise and challenge in biblical faith* (Philadelphia, PA: Fortress, 1977, 2002), p. 3.

42 Michael Moynagh, *Being Church, Doing Life* (Monarch Books, 2014), p. 272.

2 Integrating a mixed ecology

1 'How are organisms in an ecosystem interdependent? – OCR 21st Century', Bitesize, BBC, https://www.bbc.co.uk/bitesize/guides/zctwgdm/revision/5.

2 'Producers' (encyclopedic entry), National Geographic, https://education.nationalgeographic.org/resource/producers/.

3 Sarah Gibbens, 'What are wetlands, and why are they so critical for life on Earth?', 27 February 2023, https://www.nationalgeographic.co.uk/environment-and-conservation/2023/02/what-are-wetlands-and-why-are-they-so-critical-for-life-on-earth.

4 Gibbens, 'What are wetlands', 27 February 2023.

5 ChatGPT (author cannot amplify this reference).

6 Caroline Fraser, *The Crucial Role of Predators: A new perspective on ecology*, Yale Environment 360, University of Yale, 15 September 2011, https://e360.yale.edu/features/the_crucial_role_of_predators_a_new_perspective_on_ecology.

7 Graham Cray, *Mission-Shaped Church: Church planting and fresh expressions of church in a changing context* (London: Church House Publishing, 2004).

8 William Barclay, *The Letters to the Corinthians*, rev. edn (Philadelphia, PA: Westminster Press, 1975), quoted on p. 4.

9 E. Olsworth-Peter, *Mixed Ecology Learning Pathway*, Church of England, unpublished, 2021

10 Ruth Perrin and Ed Olsworth-Peter, *The Mixed Ecologists: Experiences of mixed ecology ministry in the Church of England* (London: The Archbishops Council, Church of England, 2021), https://www.churchofengland.org/sites/default/files/2021-05/focussed-study-2-the-mixed-ecologists.pdf.

11 Cathy Madavan, *Irrepressible: 12 principles for a courageous, resilient and fulfilling life* (London: SPCK, 2020).

12 Madavan, *Irrepressible*, p. 1.

13 Madavan, *Irrepressible*, p. 25.

14 Madavan, *Irrepressible*, p. 103.

15 Madavan, *Irrepressible*, p. 105.

16 E. Olsworth-Peter, *Mixed Ecology Learning Pathway*, Church of England, unpublished, 2021.

17 3D Coaching, www.3dcoaching.com.

18 'Deuteronomy 18: Priests and Prophets', Enduring Word, www.enduringword.com/bible-commentary/deuteronomy-18.

19 'A Brief History of Tents – Where Did Tents Originate? The History of Tents', *Turas: Camping and 4WD Magazine*, 14 July 2018, https://www.turas.tv/2018/07/a-brief-history-of-tents/.

20 'Dwelt: John 1:14', A Word from the Word, www.awordfromtheword.org/dwelt-john-1-14.

21 E. Olsworth-Peter, *Mixed Ecology Learning Pathway*, Church of England, unpublished, 2021.

22 Niki Segnit, *The Flavour Thesaurus: Pairings, recipes and ideas for the creative cook* (London: Bloomsbury, 2010).

23 Samuel Wells, *Incarnational Mission: Being with the world* (London: Canterbury Press, 2018), p. 12.

3 Inhabiting a mixed ecology

1 'Habitat' (encyclopedic entry), *National Geographic*, https://education.nationalgeographic.org/resource/habitat/.

2 *National Geographic*, 'Habitat'.

3 George Lings, *Seven Sacred Spaces; Portals to deeper community life in Christ* (Abingdon: BRF, 2020).

4 Lings, *Seven Sacred Spaces*.

5 E. Olsworth-Peter, *Mixed Ecology Learning Pathway*, Church of England, unpublished, 2021.

6 E. Olsworth-Peter, 'Contextual inhabitation: Exploring the 'where' of the pioneer charism', *Anvil: Journal of Theology and Mission*, Church Mission Society, vol. 35, issue 3 (October 2019).

7 E. Olsworth-Peter, 'Contextual inhabitation'.

8 E. Olsworth-Peter, *Mixed Ecology Learning Pathway*, Church of England, unpublished, 2021.

9 'About Schema Therapy', Schema Therapy Institute, https://www.schemainstitute.co.uk/understanding-schema-therapy/.

10 E. Olsworth-Peter, *Mixed Ecology Learning Pathway*, Church of England, unpublished, 2021.

11 Dwight Zscheile, 'The Culture of Innovation', lecture given at St Mellitus College, London, 16 October 2023.

12 Art of Hosting, www.artofhosting.org.

13 Harvey C. Kwiyani, *Multicultural Kingdom: Ethnic diversity, mission and the church* (London: SCM Press, 2020).

14 Anthony J. Gittins and Gerald A. Arbuckle, *Living Mission Interculturally: Faith, culture, and the renewal of praxis* (Collegeville, MN: Liturgical Press, 2015).

15 'Race: Leading a diverse Church', lecture given by Sharon Prentis at St Mellitus College, 6 November 2023.

16 Sharon Prentis, lecture given at St Mellitus, 2023.

4 Leading a mixed ecology

1 The language of seed is taken from *Encountering* The Day of Small Things (Church Army, 2017), which draws on the idea of a plant that sends seeds beyond itself, like a dandelion.

2 The language of runner is taken from *Encountering* The Day of Small Things, which draws on the idea of tubular runner roots where plants have shared roots that pop up plants in other places (think of bluebells). The only downside with this as a metaphor is that in ecclesiological terms the plants that have connected roots will often look different from one another.

3 This language was developed by the Diocese of Leicester, which

noticed that some fresh expressions that intended to be runners actually served well in growing the existing time-honoured church.

4 www.pioneer.churchmissionsociety.org/pioneer-spectrum/.

5 A generous orthodoxy argues that Jesus can be embraced across a diverse Christian landscape and through a variety of church traditions.

6 E. Olsworth-Peter, *Mixed Ecology Learning Pathway*, copyright © The Archbishops' Council 2021. Reproduced here with permission, https://www.churchofengland.org/sites/default/files/2021-05/focussed-study-2-the-mixed-ecologists.pdf.

7 Ruth Perrin and Ed Olsworth-Peter, *The Mixed Ecologists*, copyright © The Archbishops' Council 2021. Reproduced here with permission, https://www.churchofengland.org/sites/default/files/2021-05/focussed-study-2-the-mixed-ecologists.pdf.

8 Perrin and Olsworth-Peter, *The Mixed Ecologists*.

9 Mark Powley, 'The Mixed Ecologists', The Gregory Centre for Church Multiplication, October 2023, www.ccx.org.uk/content/the-mixed-ecologists.

10 The Church of England Research and Statistics, *Statistics for Mission 2019*, Church of England Mission Map, 2019, www.churchofengland.org/sites/default/files/2020-10/2019StatisticsForMission.pdf.

11 E. Olsworth-Peter, *Mixed Ecology Learning Pathway*, Church of England, unpublished, 2021.

5 Shaping a mixed ecology

1 Steve Aisthorpe, *Rewilding the Church* (Wells: St Andrew's Press, 2020).

2 Aisthorpe, *Rewilding the Church*, p. 2.

3 Tom May, *Great Ted Talks: Creativity: An unofficial guide with words of wisdom from 100 TED speakers* (Doncaster: Portico, 2020), p. 62.

4 May, *Creativity*, p. 62.

5 Lois Diamond, unpublished study notes, 2023.

6 Mel Lawrenz, *How to Understand the Bible: A simple guide* (Harrison, AR: WordWay, 2014).

7 Jonny Baker and Cathy Ross, eds., *The Pioneer Gift: Explorations in Mission* (Norwich: Canterbury Press, 2014).

8 Peter Brown, *Mr Tiger Goes Wild* (London: Two Hoots, 2017).

9 'With Great Power Comes Great Responsibility', Wikipedia, www.wikipedia.org.

10 'Stolon', Britannica, www.britannica.com/science/stolon-biology.

11 Olsworth-Peter E, *Mixed Ecology Learning Pathway*, Church of England, unpublished, 2021.

12 Eddie Newquist, '7 Characteristics of Highly Effective Innovators', Characteristics of Highly Successful Innovators, Disruptor League, 13 March 2015, https://www.disruptorleague.com/blog/2015/03/13/7-characteristics-of-highly-successful-innovators/.

13 Sarah Yardley, *More Change: Navigating change with an unchanging God* (London: SPCK, 2021), p. 56.

14 John Kotter, *The Key to Changing Organizational Culture* (Forbes, 2012).

15 Tod Bolsinger, *Canoeing the Mountains: Christian leadership in uncharted territory* (Nottingham: IVP, 2015), p. 74.

16 Bolsinger, *Canoeing the Mountains,* p. 75.

17 https://www.mindtools.com/ajm9l1e/lewins-change-management-model.

18 'Top 8 Concepts for Change Management Theory', Walk Me: The Change Management Blog, p. 23, October 2023, https://change.walkme.com/theories-of-change-management/l.

19 Samuel Wells, *Incarnational Mission: Being with the world* (Norwich: Canterbury Press, 2018).

20 Yardley, *More Change: Navigating change with an unchanging God* (London: SPCK, 2021), p. 52.

21 Yardley, *More Change.*

22 www.wackyworld.org.

23 E. Olsworth-Peter, *Mixed Ecology Learning Pathway*, Church of England, unpublished, 2021.

24 Reith Lectures, BBC iPlayer 2023, Lecture 2, released on 6 December 2023.

25 Reith Lectures, BBC iPlayer 2023, Lecture 2, released on 6 December 2023.